Contents

Foreword

After the death of our mother Hazel in 2009, shortly after she finished writing this book, we were fortunate to retrieve all of her diaries, every day from the ages of fourteen to eighty-two recorded in detail. It was a precious gift to leave behind. With her words, she brought to life the happy, the sad, the ridiculous and the magical. Christmas is a time when 'harmony and goodwill' are meant to prevail – but this does not always happen in the world of the Wheelers. *Crackers at Christmas* brings back memories of times long forgotten, including some that would perhaps be best left that way! We hope you will get as much pleasure reading it as we did.

Caroline Wilde and Elizabeth Connolly
October 2010

'Homely – the best kind of Christmas.' Christmas 1937 in the back 'living kitchen' at the shop. Pop bottle, not wine, on the table. Left to right: Hilda, Hazel, Auntie Winnie, Brian, Alice (the maid), Auntie Marion, Uncle Kenneth.

Introduction

Life is mostly froth and bubble
Two things stand alone
Kindness in another's trouble,
Courage in your own.
    Adam Lindsay Gordon, 'Ye Wearie Wayfarer'

In my diaries, besides daily happenings, I have always kept poems that appealed to me, and newspaper cuttings, to recall the passing years. And handwritten letters from friends, boyfriends – everybody!

They do help. After the death of dad, in September 1949, I copied the above. Also:

So little cause for carollings
Of such ecstatic sound,
Was written on terrestrial things,
Afar or nigh around
That I could think there trembled through,
His happy good-night air,
Some blessed Hope, whereof he knew,
And I was unaware.
    Thomas Hardy, 'The Blessed Thrush'

The very best present anyone can be given is a diary. You will be enjoying reading it every Christmas after! Sometimes days prior to Christmas have more of the atmosphere than the Big Day itself. So, here goes.

1949

A Chance Meeting

TUESDAY 6 DECEMBER

Work. Twice today two married men have asked me to go out with them – one well into his forties, the other looks about twenty-seven. They both work at David Brown's. It is very disillusioning if that is a common occurrence among married men. Told them I don't make a practice of going with other people's husbands – and one even apologised to me!

Auntie Ella came for tea and to make her initial appearance before her new brother-in-law, Syd. I went to see Dr Gilmore for how to deal with another milder lot of spots on my face. Says it's a touch of acne, and I shall have to forfeit my bacon ration, and any other fried foods for a while. Read library books *A New Conception of Love* and *Psychical Research and the Resurrection*. For the latter I require the dictionary every other word!

MONDAY 12 DECEMBER

Work. Electricity cut so Barbara, Margaret and Mrs Hartley just talked until 9.15 a.m. Another cut at 4.45 p.m. This time we were in complete darkness, so Mr Dyson allowed us to leave at 5 p.m.

Began knitting navy wool gloves for one of Syd's Christmas presents. To bed and read a chapter of *Visions of the Dying*. Couldn't sleep after for ages.

WEDNESDAY 14 DECEMBER

Evening. Stayed in with mother and Syd. Knitting gloves.

We had a good laugh over his profile in shadow on the wall, in the firelight. Greatly distorted; had him looking through a mirror at it. He thought it funny in the extreme too. Then mother and I had a turn and we all looked queer. Self-made pleasures are better than what one pays for. The wireless was good tonight, especially *Have a Go, Joe*. I coloured a photograph for a man at work.

THURSDAY 15 DECEMBER
Work. Bought Mavis a plastic red heart-shaped container with a bottle of Blue Orchid scent for her Xmas present. The boy I coloured the photograph for wanted to pay me, but I declined, with it being the first time – and nearly Christmas.

Evening. Knitting and listened to the wireless. At 9.30 p.m. Wilfred Pickles was on with a programme of poetry.

FRIDAY 16 DECEMBER
Walked home with married man Ronnie. Wanted me to go to the Ritz cinema with him. Said I was going to a dance. (But nobody to go with.)

Eventually did pluck up courage and went to Town Hall alone. As soon as I arrived on the dance floor the MC asked me for a dance, then a man excused me in the Excuse-me Quickstep. Danced with him a few times then someone else excused me. He took me to the bar for three rums and a beer. Left him when someone else danced with me. This one (he works at Brown's) came on the 1.55 a.m. last bus with me from town. Syd and Major were at Cowlersley to meet me. Glad because this fellow is always pestering me to go out with him, and I don't want to.

SATURDAY 17 DECEMBER
Busy Xmas shopping in town. Bought blue corduroy velvet coat – over £14! Coffee in Ritz café with Alastair. Met him at 5.30 p.m. to see *Easter Parade* at the Majestic. Still early when we came out so talking in Ritz café till 10 p.m. Walking home in the rain giving me a lecture – I let people get to know me too quickly, and make friends too easily etc. etc. Left him without the normal goodnight kiss – why act a comedy? Makes me feel depressed.

MONDAY 19 DECEMBER
Back early from lunch to finish putting up trimmings in the office with Barbara, Margaret and Leslie.

Evening. Listened to a play *A Winter's Tale* by Shakespeare till 11 p.m.

TUESDAY 20 DECEMBER
Work. Bought some mistletoe at lunchtime for our office. Leslie got us straightaway. (That was the intention! A kiss beneath the mistletoe with a married man is not the same as going out with him.) Charlie gave me a box of handkerchiefs for Xmas.

Evening. In from work at 5.45 p.m. Letter from Annie to meet her at 6 p.m.! What a rush. Arrived at Town Hall at 6.15 p.m. for Greenhead High School Speech Day. Saw a few of our old form mistresses of other years – many 'conspicuous by their absence' – but still a few old stagers with more grey hairs. Otherwise just the same. Home on the 9.15 p.m. trolley bus.

WEDNESDAY 21 DECEMBER

Work. Lunchtime to see Audrey and Philip. The solicitors have finished at last, and we can collect our cheques from sale of our shop. To Margaret's for tea with Barbara. Margaret lives in a 200-year-old farmhouse-type building complete with beams. All listened to a performance of the *Messiah* on wireless. Then to see the goat outside, and surrounding land. Coffee, Christmas cake and cheese at 10 p.m., then Barbara and I came home. I walked part of the way up Manchester Road before a bus came. Very enjoyable day.

FRIDAY 23 DECEMBER

Work. Was kissed under the mistletoe every few minutes. Heaven, sometimes Hell. Margaret and I stayed out at lunchtime buying goods for office party. Everybody finished about 3.15 p.m. and all sat round my desk drinking cider and eating. I got slightly merry. Walked home with Ronnie at 4.30 p.m. When we reached our gate he confessed he was going to miss me when he moved, and that he loved me and was in a terrible state. I just told him that when he was in a house alone with his wife he would think differently etc.

8 p.m. With mother and Syd for a drink in the Sportsman then to dance at St Patrick's Hall. Saw Donald, Alastair's pal. We went to a bar, and Alastair was there with Kathleen and Gerry and Betty. Tried to ignore Alastair but he came to 'have a word with me'. Danced with Donald all night. Missed last bus so he walked me home. He asked if I'd like to go to Gerry's New Year party with him. Wouldn't that be a scream? And Alastair there with another girl and me with my one-time sworn enemy!

A Happy Christmas
GOD HAVE YOU IN HIS KEEPING!

A Christmas postcard from Hazel's collection (I).

CHRISTMAS EVE

With mother to town. Deposited my cheque in Upper Aggbrig Bank. We met Syd. Lunch in restaurant the Boot and Shoe. Home for tea.

7.30 p.m. Met Philip and Audrey went to dance at St Pat's. Joined up with Andrew and Mary, who also work at the bank. It was full of scum and crowded far too much to dance. One chap kept coming to me but I sat out after being swung onto my stomach right across the floor in the Okey Cokey. Philip, Andrew and I went out in desperation for a drink. Too packed in the Sportsman to get near bar. Into the Crescent. I'd rather be out with the shepherds and sheep than *there* on a Christmas Eve.

Philip and Audrey came to bus stop with me for the 11.25. A man kept looking at me. He was next in the queue, and Philip didn't like the look of him. When I boarded the bus he came and sat by me and insisted on paying my fare, even though I had my money out. He kept trying to talk and said I 'looked well-off'. I had my new grey chinchilla fur coat on, bought from sale of our shop. At the terminus he got off too, so I went to the conductor, who was just about to go back to the depot. He told me to 'hop back on the bus and he would see me home'.

We waited along with other transport workers and they sneaked me onto the crowded last bus. The conductor's name is Granville Wheeler; he's almost twenty-two. We stood talking outside our house till about 1 a.m. He asked me to go out with him on Tuesday, but I can't. So arranged next Sunday. Granville suddenly asked me to marry him that first Christmas Eve! Chance meetings can seal one's fate for many years. Some weeks before I'd seen the same young man gazing at me on top of a bus, from the opposite side. In ordinary clothes, not a bus conductor outfit. Going down the bus steps something told me, 'You will marry that boy.' I realised when I left him and went inside the house that I'd seen him before.

I took two bulging stockings full of gifts in to mother and Syd. They were as excited as children diving down with hands discovering all the presents – including the knitted gloves, finished just in time.

CHRISTMAS DAY

Mother and I up for breakfast. Listened to the wireless.

Afternoon. Listened to the King's Christmas Day speech then packed presents in stockings for Mrs Buckley (Syd's mother), Mrs Dale (a friend of hers), Syd's sister Hilda, husband Arthur, and children Sylvia, Peter, Christine and Arthur (who later changed his name to Brian). After tea I dressed up as Father Christmas and distributed presents. Syd's other sister Doris was also there, and friend Stanley. Later I blacked out a front tooth with soot to sing 'We're a Couple of Swells' to entertain the company. One unexpected entertainment was when 'Young Arthur' pulled the chair away from Auntie Doris as she was about to sit down for the gargantuan Christmas meal in Mount Street, Lockwood. Good sport Doris – after the first stunned moment, she got up, smiled, dusted herself down and said, 'No it was only a bit of fun. Young Arthur mustn't be banished from the feast.'

Young Arthur made amends by singing 'Shake Shake the Apple Tree' afterwards. No, not in front of all those people, but from behind a curtain. And all was well that ended well. It was raining heavily when we came home on the 12 a.m. trolley.

BOXING DAY

We got up late and after dinner left home with Major to walk to town as there were queues for the trolley. On bus to Bradley Bar. Philip at football match – came back at 5 p.m. Audrey's Uncle Willie came. After tea we sat in their room, talked and ate chocolates and nuts. Left at 11 p.m. Raining again. Home on 11.25 trolley. Read in bed. Mother and Syd went to Geoffrey Davidson's wedding, then out with Hilda and Arthur. Mother said they really enjoyed themselves last night and thought I was 'a real sport'. That is thanks enough for my efforts at being a comic.

TUESDAY 27 DECEMBER

Met Mavis and went into the lounge of the George Hotel for coffee, then she came home with me for lunch. Mother and Syd took Major to relatives at Holmebridge. Mavis went to see Joseph, then Mavis, and I went to Dalton to her home for tea. I had a talk with Mrs Wise about Mavis and Joseph, and tried to put their viewpoint before her. She wants Mavis to marry 'a nice English boy', not a foreigner.

Ritz to see *Little Women* with Mavis.

WEDNESDAY 28 DECEMBER

Back to work. Walked home with Ronnie.

Lunchtime. Called to see Audrey at the National Provincial Bank and took empty bottles back from work. Stayed in and did my washing in the evening. Syd went to bed at 7 p.m. with a cold. I was in bed by 9.30 p.m. reading.

THURSDAY 29 DECEMBER

Work. Stayed in and washed my hair. Syd and mother went to the pictures. Mavis came and we talked round the fire, ate chocs and nuts, then had supper. Pleasant relaxing time, and in my favourite company, too. Mavis left at 10.15 p.m. Bed to finish reading *An Alphabet of Attributes*.

FRIDAY 30 DECEMBER

Work. Man sent me a note asking me to go out with him tomorrow. He works up one of the bays. Not keen, so I replied that I was going out. I am thinking about having a party at home and inviting some of the office people. Leslie asked if he could come – don't know whether he was joking – but it would be great fun if he would, and he wasn't flipping well married like everybody else I know.

Stayed in the evening with mother and Syd. Joseph came across for about fifteen minutes. I began knitting a mauve cardigan. Bed then to begin a library book, *Works of George Eliot*.

NEW YEAR'S EVE

Town with mother. (I took her breakfast up first.) Bought black satin cocktail dress and a purple wool one from Lucette's. Mother bought two from Marie's. Lunch in Princess Café. Home 3.45 p.m. Mother and Syd had a row. He was mad because she hadn't been home to see to his dinner – but she had left it practically ready. State of tension and suspense once more. How awful!

8.15 p.m. Met Sheila Hinchliffe, elocutionist and friend of Audrey. To Old Almondburians' dance at Albany Hall. Philip, Audrey, Mavis, Joseph, Andrew (from bank) and Mary in our party. Mainly young boys about sixteen or seventeen there: what a crew. Towards the end one young man said he would see me home, but I came home with Joseph.

Goodbye 1949 – the only fitting remark is this:

DAD – *YOU* ARE STILL MY BEST, ONE AND ONLY BOYFRIEND.

1950

Breakdown

TUESDAY 21 NOVEMBER

Afternoon. Listened to the arrival of Queen Juliana of Holland on wireless. Took Major across field to feed goats. Knitted gloves. Must give more time for presents making. People don't know the price when a gift is homemade.

WEDNESDAY 22 NOVEMBER

Shopping in town. Met mother from having her hair done. Lunch in Sylvio's. Home. Listened to the banquet in Guildhall, London, and Queen Juliana's speech. Finished gloves. Looked at fashion magazine *Harper's Bazaar*.

Evening. Drama class at Technical College. Reading J. B. Priestley's play *When We Are Married*. I read the part of Mrs Parker. Mavis now in the class with me. Granville met me outside Tech and came home with me for supper. Asking if I'd have a ring for Christmas. Mother and Syd went to see Joseph Locke at the Town Hall.

THURSDAY 23 NOVEMBER

Mother for a 'facial' at Mildred Dyson's. Met her at 11 a.m. To clinic where Mavis works. All to Fields café for lunch. Johnny, friend of Syd, called at teatime.

Evening. Met Audrey and queued outside Ritz till 8 p.m. to see Betty Hutton in *Annie Get Your Gun*. Not over till 10.45 p.m.

FRIDAY 24 NOVEMBER

Washed my hair. Johnny came and stayed till teatime as it was too bad weather for his window cleaning round. To Dr Gilmore. I begin work again on Monday after this nervous breakdown. Granville says he thinks more about me than anyone else in the world, even his own family. I'd walked with Major to his house. Margaret, his twin sister, went straight to bed. Had a cold. But that never stops my *friends* talking with me.

MONDAY 27 NOVEMBER
Recommenced work. Leslie told Barbara to give me his love. Mr Dyson sent me to see Miss Alcock, personnel officer. Both she and Dyson quite concerned about my welfare.

WEDNESDAY 29 NOVEMBER
Felt almost like old carefree times at work. Leslie teasing me about Storthes Hall (the old lunatic asylum) throughout the day. I adore his mood today. Said he would walk me up the bay as it would be the last time – they would never let me out.
    5.30 p.m. Tea with Granville in Princess Café. Met mother, Syd, and choir. By special bus to Storthes Hall. Warders followed us, locking each door as we passed through. Concert began at 7 p.m. Afterwards we had supper and speeches by a doctor, also Ronnie Daniels, the choir master. Granville came home with us. Session till 11 p.m.

THURSDAY 30 NOVEMBER
Work. Had a grand day with Leslie. I've been as unselfconscious enough today to act as silly as I used to do. I do think a lot about him – he makes me laugh so much. None more so than when we were walking up the bay and he was telling me about his Aunt Fanny. Both of us doubled up laughing and couldn't stop. If everybody could laugh like that every day, nobody would ever be depressed!

SATURDAY 2 DECEMBER
11.30 a.m. Clinic to see Mavis. Met Granville and Geoff and had coffees in Sylvio's. A lady who works with them at Hopkinson's joined us. Stayed there talking till nearly 1 p.m. Buying Christmas presents. With Granville. Spent ages (and almost £8 at Rushworth's cosmetics counter). Home 3.15 p.m. Had a bath and tried new Blue Grass talcum powder.

SUNDAY 3 DECEMBER
Coloured a photo. Granville came; walked to their house for tea. Slippery as it had snowed. His Auntie Evelyn there. Granville and I went to Linthwaite Chapel. Both fell, and bumped our heads together. Also I broke one of my favourite yellow flower earrings. Back to Gran's for supper.

WEDNESDAY 6 DECEMBER
Work. Raining in afternoon, clearing away the snow. Electric cut from 4 p.m. till we left work. I was by Leslie all the time – and he acted the fool as usual. Asked me

about having a night out with him etc. Tech at night. Reading the play *Laburnum Grove*. Granville met me; home for supper. He's wanting me to say I love him. I'll be engaged, and so forth, more than ever.

THURSDAY 7 DECEMBER
Work. Lunch in Collinson's with mother and Margaret.

Evening. To Hopkinson's dance with Granville. Wore my evening dress. We had rums first in the Wellington. Met Geoff and his friend Mavis at Cambridge Baths. Six or seven more rums there. I didn't enjoy myself. Crowded, no one there of any momentum. Just a crush of silly humanity. Far more fun with Leslie and no drinks at all. Home in taxi at midnight. Granville proposing marriage practically all the time.

FRIDAY 8 DECEMBER
Hilarious day at work. Mr Dyson must think I am the ringleader as he rang for me and told me I was one of the culprits and if we didn't quieten down I'd 'get my marching orders'.

SATURDAY 9 DECEMBER
Coffee with Margaret Sykes in Fields café. Shopping with her till 1.30 p.m. Knitting gloves for Granville this afternoon. He called for me at 6 p.m. Bus to town then walked to Moldgreen Church to see *The Pirates of Penzance*. Home and talked over our ideal partnerships for marriage – and what type of life we would want – something we can't ask Father Christmas for!

SUNDAY 10 DECEMBER
2.15 p.m. Granville came and we drank coffee and discussed with mother what we would like for Christmas. To Auntie Annie's for tea, then to hear the *Messiah* at Moldgreen Chapel. So crowded we had to sit on chairs in the aisles. Back home, supper, and listened to a play in the firelight.

MONDAY 11 DECEMBER
Another good day at work. I'm practically cured of the 'hot and bothered' feeling now, and am back to my old standard of supplying a laugh a minute to the other office members.

Evening. Had a rum in the White Hart with mother, then met Annie Whitworth and she went with us to the *Messiah* rehearsal. Hope she didn't smell our breath.

TUESDAY 12 DECEMBER
Work. Walked down fields home for lunch. Tea in canteen with Margaret and Hilton. Worked over with Leslie and the others. I asked Leslie if I could see him once a week if I married (to have a laugh). That made him laugh, and he said, 'Can you buggery!'

A Christmas postcard from Hazel's collection (II).

Left work at 7.30 p.m. Walked home. Mother and Syd have bought me half a dozen wine glasses for Christmas.

WEDNESDAY 13 DECEMBER

This afternoon Mr Dyson had me in his office because I'd put a wrong address on a label. It upset me quite a lot. Laughing again going up bay with Leslie afterwards.

Evening. Technical College. Read the poem 'On His Blindness' by John Milton. Mrs Whitfield complimented me on my reading. Then I had the main part in a play. Granville met me outside Tech. Hand in hand to bus. Home for supper. Listened to *Have a Go, Joe*.

THURSDAY 14 DECEMBER

Snow. No electricity at work till after lunch. Leslie, Herbert and the ordinary workers came at 9.30 a.m. Before they arrived, Barbara, Margaret and I put Xmas trimmings round the office.

Lunch in Collinson's with mother, Marjorie and Mavis. Finished work 3.30 p.m. Electric cut off again. We chanted a poem: 'Living in the jungle/Candles in the hut/ Better than electric/No cut.' Walked home in the snow.

Stayed in all evening knitting gloves and writing Christmas cards.

FRIDAY 15 DECEMBER
Work till 5.15 p.m. With Barbara and Margaret for a turkey tea at the Pack Horse. No one else in and we laughed non-stop. The tea was grand, trifle afterwards, then to the play *A Christmas Carol* at the Theatre. Granville met us at 9.15 p.m. and took the three of us for coffee in the Ritz café. He came back home for supper. Had a thoroughly enjoyable evening – every minute, every second.

SATURDAY 16 DECEMBER
Shopping. Met Gran.
   11.45 a.m. Saw Alastair. We said 'good morning' as we passed in the crowd.
   At 4 p.m. we went to his Auntie Evelyn's for tea.
   Knitting and listening to records in evening, and talking. Walked home with Gran.

SUNDAY 17 DECEMBER
8 a.m. Having to go to work. Got lift in a milk float (wearing fur coat too!).
   At 12 noon I went to St Luke's Hospital with Mrs Hartley to see her husband. Talked to him and a Polish boy who has consumption of the kidneys. Leslie had put a Christmas card in my drawer this morning.
   To Granville's for tea. Stayed in their house with the others, put trimmings up and knitted.

MONDAY 18 DECEMBER
Work. Leslie is away with influenza. I am very chagrined that it should happen just at this time. There is a piece of mistletoe hanging over my desk – and I *was* hoping that I could kiss 'Diddums'.
   [Here is a poem I either wrote or copied, dedicated to Diddums, who used to share my morning elevenses – then a carrot or two.]

   The Gift
   Say, cruel Diddums, handsome rake,
      Dear mercenary beauty, what daily offering shall I make
         Expression of my duty?
            My carrot, a victim to thine eyes, should I at once deliver,
         Say, would the greedy witty one prize the gift, who scorns the giver?
            A cigarette, chewing gum, sweets or toy –
   The others give – and let 'em. If those to you impart a joy,
      I'll give them – when I get 'em.
         I'll give, but not the full-blown rose, or rosebud, more in fashion,
   Such short-lived offerings but disclose a transitory passion.
            I'll give thee something yet unpaid, not less sincere than civil,
      I'll give thee – yes: too charming male –
         I'll give thee – to the Devil!

[Another poem dedicated to Diddums in my 1950 diary was based on 'To Phoebe' by W. S. Gilbert.]

'Smiles that thrill from any distance
Shed upon me while I sing!
Please ecstaticise existence,
Love me, oh thou fairy thing!'
Words like these, outpouring sadly,
You'd perpetually hear,
If I loved you, fondly, madly –
But I do not, Diddums dear.

TUESDAY 19 DECEMBER
Work. Very tame without my old pal 'Diddums'. No interest in the mistletoe whatsoever now.

5.15 p.m. Ran most of the way home from work. Changed into my new navy and white dress, town for 6.15 p.m. Met Granville, Geoff, and Joyce Cowling in the Ritz café. Coffee and cakes before going on to Hopkinson's Drawing Office dinner at Whiteley's café. Boiled ham etc., three various trifles, cakes and tea. One or two speeches – by the way the tables were lit by candlelight – games, dancing. Also there was a conjuror, and a quartet to sing for us. Had a good evening, finishing there at 10.30 p.m. Granville brought me home.

WEDNESDAY 20 DECEMBER
Work.

Evening. Technical College, only five of us there. Read play *Hewers of Coal* then adjourned to the staff room where we had coffee, biscuits and conversation. Mrs Whitfield said that I would be very good if I joined a dramatic society (i.e. a good actress, not morally!).

Mavis and I then to carol concert in the Fraternity Hall. Mother, Syd and Mrs Buckley there.

THURSDAY 21 DECEMBER
Work. All had rum in our coffee and Xmas cake. And mince pies, which Barbara's mother had made. Very busy all day – not bothered either, as Leslie is absent.

Stayed in all evening. Washed a couple of dresses, then packed Christmas presents in stockings for mother and Syd.

FRIDAY 22 DECEMBER
Should have met Barbara at 10.30 a.m. but didn't awake till then. Town later. Lunch with Mavis in Fields café. Called to see Audrey at bank. Shopping till 4 p.m. Granville came in the evening. Syd took Major to vet as he has eczema on

his back again. Mother stayed in with us. All listened to the Huddersfield Choral Society, who were broadcasting the *Messiah*.

SATURDAY 23 DECEMBER
Very cold, frosty, layer of snow. Town. Coffee in Fields café.

10.30 a.m. With Granville. Shopping. Called at Thornton Lodge to see Jeanne. With her, Norman, and Granville to the Empire cinema. Jeanne's for supper. Stayed till 12 p.m. Home on trolley.

CHRISTMAS EVE
Gran came after dinner. Snowing. To G.'s for tea. Mavis, Joseph, Annie Whitworth, Philip and Audrey, Jeanne and Norman there afterwards. Played games, sang carols round the piano. After supper the men played cards; we preferred to talk. Home by taxi at 12.30 a.m. Then Gran and I watched mother and Syd open their stockings before Granville walked all the way back after we'd ridden in the taxi. Poor thing.

CHRISTMAS DAY
All got up late. Helping mother all afternoon preparing for Syd's relatives from Lockwood. Also Thornton Lodge. Brian Gibson, one of his friends from work, also came. Granville arrived about 4 p.m. Played games after tea. All four children of Hilda and Arthur's here. Absolute Bedlam. Would prefer a good book! When they all went, Granville, Brian, Syd, mother and I played cards.

BOXING DAY
Granville came in the afternoon. We walked via canal bank to his house with Major. Mr and Mrs Wheeler and Margaret went out for tea. Granville and I brought large armchair (for two) into the kitchen and listened to the wireless and had a long passionate few hours before tea, which we had at 7.30 p.m. We are thinking about going abroad next year, touring. He suggested our getting engaged in Venice.

WEDNESDAY 27 DECEMBER
Work. We have a new fifteen-year-old junior in the office, Pat Mosley. Leslie has now got yellow jaundice and goodness knows when we'll see him again. Stayed in and washed clothes after tea. Syd and mother poor company tonight. But mother has a bad cold – that is the reason for her quietness. Gentleman who works at Brook Motors gave me a lift to work in his car this morning. Asked me to go out with him. Refused.

THURSDAY 28 DECEMBER
Work. Took some port wine and Barbara, Margaret, Pat and I had a 'drinking bout' in the middle of the afternoon. Pat informs me that she likes me the best in the office!

Evening. Met Annie Whitworth and David (tenor) and another member of the choir and had a rehearsal of the *Messiah* in Moldgreen Parish Church. Home on 10 p.m. trolley by myself. Syd has got a cold; has not been to work today. How I *do* wish 'Diddums' was back.

FRIDAY 29 DECEMBER
Work.

Evening. Granville came at 7 p.m. and we went to the Princess pictures. Syd and mother staying in, and when those two and Major are congregated round the fire – which is in the corner of the room – we two haven't a chance.

I told Granville tonight that I too loved him. Somehow I feel as if I do now, I suppose time is performing as with Alastair and he is 'growing' on my affections. But he had a better start than Al!

SATURDAY 30 DECEMBER
Town with mother. Met Granville and Geoffrey. Coffee in Sylvio's. Gran came back home with us for dinner. Stayed all day. We sat in the front room after tea with mother and Syd. Looked at photographs, played cards, read diary together. Granville left to walk home about one in the morning. Never know if he arrives alright.

NEW YEAR'S EVE
Stayed in bed reading till teatime. Granville came. He and Syd, Mrs Buckley, Sylvia and Christine – Syd's nieces – came to Moldgreen Parish Church with us. The Co-op choir gave the *Messiah*. I sat next to Annie. Gran came back home with us. He caught last bus.

So ends 1950. On the whole, quite an agreeable year. There have been 'ups and downs' but I cannot grumble. And another year nearer dad.

Can't grumble at that either.

1951

Engagement

SUNDAY 9 DECEMBER
Hailing, blowing, snowing and all sorts of weather. Yesterday some coal slack, which mother paid £1 for, was all washed away down the drain! Rushing to knit Granville a pullover for Christmas. When mother and Syd went to Mrs Buckley's for tea we forgot knitting till 5.30 p.m. then made tea for two. Granville left at 9.30 p.m. I finished a sleeve by 11.15 p.m.

MONDAY 10 DECEMBER
Work. Stayed in by myself in the evening. Wrote paragraph for *Examiner*. Knitting pullover. The first snow of the winter. It looked like Christmas at last.

WEDNESDAY 12 DECEMBER
Shall be very annoyed tomorrow if we don't receive rise in wages in lieu of increased cost of living. Tech. Read a part in the play. Made them laugh. Christine and another girl said I was very good at acting.

THURSDAY 13 DECEMBER
We didn't receive the expected rise in wages. An electricity cut; all sitting in the dark. Then I had a big row with that despicable personage, Raymond. Indeed, not a very delightful thirteenth. The weather didn't improve matters – a blanket of thick fog. Knitted this evening.

SATURDAY 15 DECEMBER
To Annie's with Granville for the evening. The silly twirp presented him with a bar of cleaning soap, a knitted dishcloth, and a plate mop for washing up! I haven't

1951 Christmas card from Granville to Hazel.

felt as embarrassed and at a loss for words for ages. I don't think Granville has either. Home on 10.30 trolley.

SUNDAY 23 DECEMBER

To Granville's on trolley. He smoked large fat cigars and we had some tea and Christmas cake before coming home at 10 p.m.

CHRISTMAS EVE

With Granville on train to Leeds. Pouring with rain. Turkey lunch in Lewis'. Granville's for tea. Met Mavis and Joseph and Philip.

7.30 p.m. Audrey didn't come as it was raining. The Queen for a couple of drinks. Philip, Granville and I up to Bradley Bar at 9 p.m. Mrs Cudworth hardly spoke. Philip played Hell about her. Gran thought I wasn't going to give him a Christmas stocking; was surprised when told it was reposing on his bed at his home.

CHRISTMAS DAY

Mother and I deploring this day, I suppose because of the upset on Saturday. Syd told mother Philip had *not* to come to *his* house on Xmas Day. I'd invited them as he and mother were going out. I'd felt like David Copperfield probably felt with his

A Christmas postcard from Hazel's collection (III).

stepfather, and retaliated by saying *he* hadn't any principles, seeing mother before dad died. Had to dash outside; thought he was going to hit me. *Merry Xmas?*

I didn't want to go to Wheeler's; would have preferred Philip and Audrey. But went for a walk with Granville first before the Windrams arrived there. They were nicer than I imagined they'd be. After a tremendous dinner, they all played cards. Wished they hadn't to leave before 6 p.m. because of their daughter's baby. I knitted, having had enough of cards. *They* played till 11 p.m.

BOXING DAY
After dinner to Granville's; glad they had all gone out. He was making a cushion cover while I knitted his pullover and listened to the wireless. His twin Margaret returned at 9 p.m. crying. Said she felt ill and upset. I felt very sorry, but couldn't do anything as she wouldn't say what had upset her.

THURSDAY 27 DECEMBER
Back to work. Knitted pullover and read Charles Dickens.

SATURDAY 29 DECEMBER
8.30 a.m. Work till 12 noon. Walked home. Trolley to Granville's. In taxi with all his family to Mrs Windram's at Beaumont Park. Drank sherry and talked till

teatime. Turkey, pork etc. etc. Afterwards – played cards. Wish cards had never been invented. Supper. Home in taxi at midnight.

SUNDAY 30 DECEMBER
Knitting after breakfast. (Who invented knitting?) Granville came at 2.15 p.m. Town to meet Mavis and Joseph. To her house for tea. Three friends of hers, Jock, Doreen and Michael, were there. Played 'Twenty Questions' and then a general knowledge quiz. Home on 10 p.m. bus from Dalton.

NEW YEAR'S EVE
This will be the last entry in this book for 1951. Spent the day at work, walked home 5.15 p.m. Mother and Syd went to the pictures. Granville came and had a bath. (He usually goes to his Auntie Nellie's next door; they haven't a bathroom at 2 Lowestwood.) We sat in the kitchen over a fire that wouldn't blaze, and I knitted while we talked.

Towards the end of this year I really took the plunge and accepted an engagement ring from Granville. That, I believe, is the biggest step this year. To what – who knows? – but I feel sure that with Granville I will be made happy.

My New Year Resolution shall be a renewal of a pledge I made to myself and the memory of dad. To behave as kindly to *my* future husband as dad did to mother, and never, never, to let him down. I fall far short of that ideal, which is ever-present in my mind. I'm jealous and suppose at times argumentative too. But I hope I will grow out of this phase.

One *good* point in Granville's favour: I only become unreasonably jealous when I care!

Well, roll in 1952. Is it really me, Hazel Taylor, wishing that before next New Year's Eve I shall be put to the test, to see how I fare as the wife of Granville Wheeler?

Not on speaking terms with Syd yet. I'd love to entertain people, especially Philip and Audrey, in a home of our own. Preparing all manner of fantastic banquets amid lovely surroundings, for those I want to be near. Mmm – the idea is scrumptious! Perhaps the cakes won't be, but it should be *great fun*. I'm looking forward to it. And I love GW too, really 100 per cent – but I wish that he could spell a little better.

The Spirit of Christmas Past

I bought a 1927 *Methodist Times* for Christmas 1927 at a book fair. The year I was born. It shows the true Christmas Spirit in these mercenary times.

That year donations sent to the Rev. F. W. Chudleigh, at Stepney Central Hall, helped provide 1,500 parcels for poor homes where there would be little Christmas cheer. In 1927, 10s paid for a parcel of Christmas 'goodies', and every child could choose a toy from Santa Claus. Horace was one of those poor children. His dad was out of work, and his little sister Annie was ill in bed, so she couldn't claim a ticket for a present from Father Christmas.

How Horace envied youngsters coming out of a toy shop, laden with toys. Not for himself, but for Annie. At the party for poor children, Horace saw a little girl being given a doll. To the astonishment of Santa, Horace gave his ticket and asked for a doll too.

'What do you want a doll for, laddie?' asked the whiskery figure.

Horace didn't reply. But for the first time that Christmas in 1927, 'Unlucky Horace', as he considered himself, had a bit of luck. When he went back home, he gave the doll to Annie and saw her face! Sheer delight – that was enough for Horace.

Ideal gifts for youngsters not reliant on charity were *Monster* annuals, *Boys' Own* annuals (12s 6d) and *Girls' Own* annuals (also 12s 6d). They contained over 700 large pages of reading and pictures, coloured 'plates' and 1,000 other illustrations. Compare those 'bumper' annuals to the expensive, anorexic-looking specimens available in 2008. Those books celebrated England and the Empire. Children were proud to be English. The *School Boys' Annual* (3s 6d) had nineteen stories of pluck and adventure. The *School Girls' Annual* had similar content.

The Methodist Times,
vol. XLIII, no. 2,239.

 No wonder children could read better in 1927 than they can today, despite technology. Perhaps it was because they didn't sit all day staring at the TV, where names do not even have capital letters. How delightful *my* 1930s Christmases were, when I would lie in front of a blazing log fire with a new annual on the rug in front of me.

 How to Sleep on a Windy Night with an introduction by the Rev. Mark Guy Pearse (2s 6d) was one of the gift-type books of 1927. *Ever – A Child's Book of Joy* (2s 6d) was 'for those who would learn how to talk to children about death and immortality'.

 Today, children talk about sex and drugs, and know hardly anything about what really matters in life. They may think they have it all, but in reality they are more deprived than those 'slum' children of 1927.

 One heart-rending advert in the *Methodist Times* reads, 'Forgotten! Did you ever as a child wake up on a Christmas morning to find your stocking empty? The pale-faced slum child believes in Santa Claus and wistfully looks for him, but, alas, many are terribly disappointed. Thousands attended the Slum Children's Service at the Deptford Mission.'

 The Rev. Harold Westlake appealed to readers to remember the Christmas Cheer Fund, which provided 'Special Treats and Entertainments' for thousands of

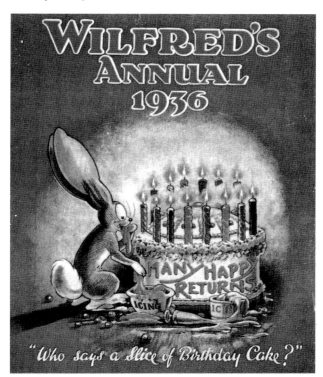

Wilfred, the son of Pip and Squeak, gorges on icing on the front cover of his 1936 annual.

children, parties for the poor, tired, aged mothers and cripples, parcels of groceries for needy families, coals for empty grates, food for empty cupboards, toys for empty stockings, joy for empty lives, and Christmas cheer for all. Readers were invited to send a postcard for the Deptford Mission Christmas story entitled 'Christmas Eve in Christie's Court'.

Spending Christmas in a children's home in 1927 was probably infinitely more rewarding than the ones spent by the materialistic generation of today. Few know the true meaning of Christmas, can't be bothered to go to a church service, and 'couldn't care less' as long as *they* have enough to eat – and drink.

The Rev. John H. Litten had an article published in the *Methodist Times* on 8 December 1927 – 'Christmas in the Children's Home'. It read, 'After the joy of opening stockings follows morning service where children's voices join in Christmas hymns of thanksgiving for the greatest Christmas gift of all. Then a walk before Christmas dinner. All the time-honoured customs duly observed.' Later in the day there was a Christmas concert, which the children themselves provided. 'Then presently to the end of a perfect day, weary but content.'

I look back wishfully to the delightful music – as opposed to non-stop 'pop' – of those early twentieth century Christmases. A Saturday popular concert on 10 December 1927 at Kingsway Hall included the Roosters Concert Party: 'Cathcart

Lynn, contralto, Harry Brindle, bass, Carlos Ames, harp soloist, Frederick Lennard, humorist, Gatty Bellars, organ solos, George Ison, accompanist. Prices 3*s*, 2*s*, 1*s* 6*d* and 1*s*, numbered and reserved. 6*d* unreserved.'

Jokes were not 'smutty'. For example:

> 'Your brother went abroad on a Fellowship, didn't he?' asked the chatty young man.
>
> 'No,' was the reply. 'It was a cattle ship.'

At the annual Christmas dinner of a farmers' club, the carver of a huge turkey asked the waiter to inquire of each committee man what portion he would like before he started carving. Each man professed a desire to have a leg. At this the carver was somewhat confused. Rising, he exclaimed, 'Gentlemen, I should like to oblige you all, but this is a turkey I'm carving, not a blessed spider.'

Lantern slides added to the enjoyment of Christmas. The Wesleyan Methodist Sunday School Dept at Ludgate Circus House had 'a splendid range of microscopes, lanterns, and other optical goods. And a magnificent range of slides on all subjects, will gladly quote terms for hiring.'

Where today in a magazine could be found a Sunday School column?

The National Children's Home and Orphanage had a poem by Edna Norman in the *Methodist Times*, 'Christmas Candles':

> All ye who Christians be,
> Oh, light my tiny candle here for me,
> It has gone out, I am not very old,
> And as I travelled in the cold
> A bitter wind with all his might
> Blew, and put out my little light.
>
> All ye who Christians be,
> Will ye not list to me,
> Who have so often prayed
> I might not be afraid?
> I am a little frightened – can't you see?
> Oh, light my little candle here for me.

By sending five guineas a secure immediate admission for 'One of These Little Ones' was assured.

During 1927, 731 children had already been received into the Children's Home and there was still a waiting list of 142 more.

There can never be perfection, but at least in the early years of the century we didn't hear anyone complaining of being bored. There were choir rehearsals to go to, knitting to be done for the poor besides one's family, Christmas decorations to make, holly to be gathered from the hedgerows, wood to be gathered for winter kindling, Christmas cakes to help stir and wish 'good luck' to as they went into the oven, mince pies to bake (how much more interesting than buying them ready-made!), puzzles to solve in annuals, and pine cones to gather for decorating the house. There was also a musical parcel to make for a Christmas party – layer after layer of papers were wrapped around the small gift inside, which was passed round while mother played the piano, stopping every so often for another layer of paper to be torn off.

The *Methodist Times* ran a competition – 'How to Make Home Happiest at Christmas'. The half-guinea prize was awarded to a Mrs A. Michelson of Stockport, who ended her letter, 'See that the skeleton cupboard is securely locked, and all private grievance hid away out of sight under the carpet. Thus, if you give of the best you have to give, the best will come back to you, and when you seek your rest from the toil of happy care, you will be certain it was worthwhile the expense and excitement of entertaining a Royal Guest.'

We can still learn a lot about living from those who lived before. Especially about how to have a Happy Christmas.

1958

Dog on Wheels

SATURDAY 13 DECEMBER

At dinnertime Granville fell down the cellar steps and bruised his spine. He was trying to escape from the coal man, who wanted paying. I want shopping by myself in the afternoon. G. went to the infirmary after, and came back in an ambulance. He has to go for an X-ray on Monday.

Evening. Wrapping presents and knitting.

MONDAY 15 DECEMBER

9 a.m. Ambulance took Granville for X-ray. He didn't come back till 1.30 p.m. They carried him upstairs to bed. He has to lie flat on a board for a week.

Afternoon. Making lemon cheese with Elizabeth. At teatime Pamela from next door came to play with them. She then took Elizabeth in to watch their TV. I went to the bread shop in fog. Pamela's dad came in to help me move furniture and get single bed downstairs for Granville. We put his board on it, then they lent us some blankets.

Evening. Dusting, seeing to Granville, knitting, writing letters.

TUESDAY 16 DECEMBER

Took Elizabeth and Caroline to Aspley Post Office in a car from Granville's work. One of the office girls had been driven up. To town to buy crackers, hot water bottle for Norman, magazines.

WEDNESDAY 17 DECEMBER

I moved furniture by myself again to put bed near the window. Just having dinner when Norman, the Indian bus conductor, came. He stayed while I went to shop, starting work at 4 p.m.

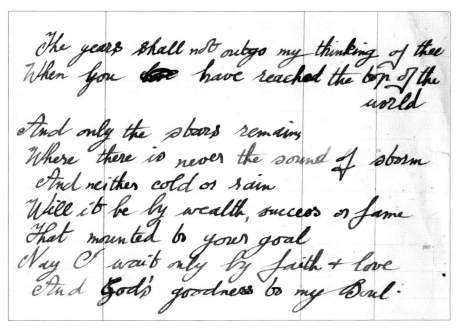

The years shall not outgo my thinking of thee
When you have reached the top of the world

And only the stars remain
Where there is never the sound of storm
And neither cold or rain
Will it be by wealth, success or fame
That mounted to your goal
Nay I wait only by faith + love
And God's goodness to my Soul:

The epigraph from Ethel M. Dell's *The Top of the World*. Transcribed in 1958 with Granville in mind.

Then Mrs Wheeler came. Stayed for tea. Granville wanted a jam jar* while she was here. She hung tablecloth over table so no one would see him, but it kept slipping so she planted a packet of Demerara sugar on it. Then, when coming downstairs after emptying it, Elizabeth said, 'Where have you been?'

Mrs W. said, 'Daddy's been to the toilet.'

TUESDAY 23 DECEMBER

Afternoon. Shopping in town. Pamela playing with E. and C. I called at Kaye's to see if Granville had ordered the right walking doll. He hadn't – I felt almost sick, then they said they only had one more left – at three guineas. Ordered that, then 'flew' to Barker's to see if they had any cheaper ones, then to Henry's. They are putting two on one side till the morning.

Evening. Expecting chap to bring Granville's wage. He didn't arrive. I baked.

CHRISTMAS EVE

A man from work took me to town in his car to collect walking doll, dog on wheels, and other toys. He brought them back; hid them in the hut. I went to

---

*It's unclear what Granville is up to here. Presumably his accident means he has to use a jar to relieve himself – with much difficulty.

Elizabeth and Caroline.

Heywood's and signed up for a record player on HP terms. Called for large pork pie, ginger wine etc. Mr Evans brought me back in van with record player. Then I had to dash back again for bread.

Afternoon. Children's party. Pamela, Doreen, her little girl Christine, and another two-year-old called Christine came. We played the new Xmas records a lot.

Evening. Annie came with presents. Supper in front room.

CHRISTMAS DAY
Morning. Elizabeth and Caroline opened their stockings in our bed. Then they played with new things in front room. Pamela came in for a while.

Afternoon. Preparing tea. Mother and Syd came, then Norman at about 6.15 p.m. In the evening Philip and Audrey, Jeanne and Norman. We played my 'Christmas Casual' recording among others, and had a candlelight supper. Philip and Audrey didn't leave till about 1.30 a.m.

BOXING DAY
Afternoon. Playing with E. and C. dressing dolls, blow football, new jigsaw. Annie came to tea. She did jigsaw with Granville and Elizabeth. Evening: knitting, talking, eating horse chestnuts. Supper.

Elizabeth (five), Caroline (three), and the
'dog on wheels', August 1959.

SATURDAY 27 DECEMBER
Afternoon. To mother's Christmas party with Granville, Elizabeth, Caroline,
Auntie Annie. Philip, Audrey, Shirley and Mrs Cudworth came to tea, too. Played
games in front room, back in taxi at 8 p.m. Syd gave us a lot of records, which we
brought back. Read papers.

MONDAY 29 DECEMBER
Washing.
    Afternoon. Granville to doctor's. Ironed, then played ambulances with Elizabeth
and Caroline. Then read *Andy Pandy* in front of the fire.

TUESDAY 30 DECEMBER
After dinner Granville went to infirmary for check-up. Elizabeth pushed Caroline
on her dog on wheels most of the way to call and see Auntie Annie's Christmas
cards. Nobody else had been. Elizabeth had a few rides coming back via Spider
Alley.

NEW YEAR'S EVE
Morning. Making dinner etc. Caroline on 'dog on wheels' again. Down Spider
Alley to Ravensknowle Park. Picked sticks of wood for fire. Called at grocer's.
Mother waiting outside house when we got back. We played records for her then
had tea.
    Evening. She cleaned kitchen for me, then read to Elizabeth. Mrs Williamson
called in to see if either of us would like to go into their New Year's Eve party.
Mother went home at 9.30 p.m. Granville went next door at 11.30 p.m., staying
at their party till the early hours. I felt, as usual, more than a little sad at the
passing of something that can never come again. Went to bed about 12.30 a.m.
and lay listening to the 'comings and goings' of the people next door.

1959

No Fury Like a
Woman Scorned

MONDAY 21 DECEMBER

Mother here. Two men came from Heywood's again. Shopping in town. Spent my money from *Weekend* on a Popeye for Caroline. Also bought a *Watch with Mother* book, felt, and blunt scissors for Elizabeth. And a pair of long scarlet socks each. Mother said two men had been because Granville still owes television firm over £8. He never mentioned anything to me. I was furious.

Evening. Blowing balloons up, wrapping E. and C.'s presents. Knitting and watching *Probation Officer*.

TUESDAY 22 DECEMBER

Shops with E. and C. Dolls, pram, and walking doll.

Afternoon. Sticking blobs of cotton wool on windows for 'snow', blowing up balloons etc. They watched *Andy Pandy*. Granville to Pack Horse. Just finished reading story to Elizabeth when doorbell rang. Then back door, then banging at living-room windows. Two men to take away the television because G. still hasn't paid. One of the men who knew him said he couldn't understand Granville – and wondered what his family would think. I finished sewing up jumper, and read papers in complete silence after E. went to sleep.

THURSDAY 24 DECEMBER

Town again for last shopping. Coffee in Whiteley's. Caroline had an ice cream, Elizabeth a drink of orange.

Afternoon. Linda Ramsden, Elizabeth's friend at school, Janet Venables and little Christine came to the party. Janet brought a box of paints, Linda a small book. Mother came and amused them while I prepared tea.

For table cover, lengths of crimson and green crêpe paper. Parents called for them about 7 p.m. Granville went to Pack Horse. Mother to meet Syd. I tidied up, did piles of washing up. Took pillow cases into bedroom and put the two drums, dolls' house and pram in front room.

CHRISTMAS DAY

Elizabeth woke about 5 a.m. All in our bed looking at presents. Janet came to show her scooter. Mr and Mrs Wheeler, mother and Syd came. They all played in front room with E. and C. Left before 10 p.m. Mother and Syd last after talking and sherry. Syd had a cigar.

BOXING DAY

Pouring with rain.

Afternoon. To Kathleen Driver's cottage at Dogley, near Kirkburton, for tea. With Granville, Elizabeth and Caroline. For a bit of fun Kathleen sat on Granville's knee – and Caroline first burst into tears then flew at her in a blind rage!

Kathleen did laugh, saying, 'No fury like a woman scorned.' Watched her TV then home and Granville to Pack Horse.

SUNDAY 27 DECEMBER

All to mother's for tea. Auntie Annie, Syd's sister Doris, a friend Brian Gibson and his girlfriend also there. Elizabeth and Caroline enjoyed playing tiddlywinks.

MONDAY 28 DECEMBER

Mrs Wheeler 'phoned to play pop because Margaret hadn't received a card. Granville, so he said, must have put the wrong number on. He went to Pack Horse in the evening. I read to Elizabeth and Caroline. Finished ironing (till next time).

TUESDAY 29 DECEMBER

Stayed in all day. Raining. Elizabeth and Caroline playing with dolls' house, pram etc.

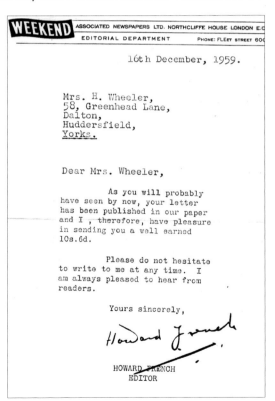

WEEKEND ASSOCIATED NEWSPAPERS LTD. NORTHCLIFFE HOUSE LONDON E.C

EDITORIAL DEPARTMENT   PHONE: FLEET STREET 600

16th December, 1959.

Mrs. H. Wheeler,
58, Greenhead Lane,
Dalton,
Huddersfield,
Yorks.

Dear Mrs. Wheeler,

As you will probably have seen by now, your letter has been published in our paper and I, therefore, have pleasure in sending you a well earned 10s.6d.

Please do not hesitate to write to me at any time. I am always pleased to hear from readers.

Yours sincerely,

HOWARD FRENCH
EDITOR

Editor Howard French pays Hazel for her contribution to *Weekend*, 16 December 1959.

ESTABLISHED 1850   **5034**

BARKER'S *of Huddersfield*

(PROPRIETORS JOSEPH BARKER LTD.)

SPORTS OUTFITTERS · TOYS · TRAVEL GOODS

CORNER HOUSE
MARKET PLACE
TEL · 1212

DIRECTORS :
MR. J. R. BARKER
MRS. A. BARKER
MISS P. M. BARKER
GEN. MANAGER :
A. T. CORMACK

M. _Mrs. Wheeler_

58 Greenland Lane
Bolton

Date _23/11/59_   Assistant _Be._

May Box			5	11
Basket Making			4	6
Loom			10	—
Jigsaw			3	11
		1	4	4
Deposit Paid			4	
Bal to pay		1	—	4

Paid

Receipt for Christmas presents
purchased in Barker's,
23 November 1959.

Afternoon. Read stories to them. I dressed all the dolls and the teddy bear, and put Walking Doll's hair in paper curlers. Wrote and typed readers' letters. Outstanding bills, including for the now missing television, to pay.

WEDNESDAY 30 DECEMBER
Town with E. and C. Mother's for dinner. Syd at home – bronchitis. He played dominoes with Elizabeth. We watched Bill and Ben. Home before dark for tea, Played games in front room with Elizabeth and Caroline.

NEW YEAR'S EVE
Caroline had earache but insisted she felt fit enough to go to Jeanne's. When there she just slept on my knee, cried, and wouldn't eat or drink anything. Elizabeth had fun playing with Diane. Home 7 p.m. Betty and her friend Doris came. We sat in front room talking. Granville to Pack Horse. It's to be hoped the 1960s are an improvement on recent years. This 1959 diary cost 4s, including Purchase Tax.

1960

Completely Crackers

TUESDAY 20 DECEMBER

Shops at Waterloo with Caroline.

Afternoon. Elizabeth's party at school, so took Caroline to see Father Christmas in town. Christmas present shopping afterwards. Met Elizabeth at 4 p.m. She'd made another little funny hat and their Father Christmas had given them crayons. She still ate more tea when we came home.

Evening. Granville to Marriage Guidance.

WEDNESDAY 21 DECEMBER

10.30 a.m. School to watch Elizabeth in Christmas play and carols. Caroline sat on the floor at the front with Miss Taylor. Mother was there

Afternoon. Shopping in town by myself. Caroline at home with mother.

Evening. Granville to Stag as usual.

THURSDAY 22 DECEMBER

Afternoon. Town with Caroline. I paid for a record they had made.

3.30 p.m. Met Elizabeth who has now broken up for Xmas holidays. She has made a spill holder with six spills in it for Granville and a calendar for me.

Evening. Knitting dolls' bootees. Jeanne came with presents.

FRIDAY 23 DECEMBER

Cleaning bedrooms, bathroom and stairs. Elizabeth and Caroline playing together.

Evening. Watching *Alice in Wonderland* with them, then Charlie Drake. After they had gone to bed, I ironed then knitted another doll's cap. Granville to Stag.

ELIZABeth wheeler
christmas Holidays.
We brek up at 330.pm
on Thursday 22nd.
December We come
back to school on
Wednesday 11th January

Elizabeth's memo to self, 22 December 1960.

CHRISTMAS EVE

Shopping in town with G., E. and C. We had coffee in Rushworth's. Granville refused to come into the toy department with us and waited outside.

Afternoon. Baking mince pies etc.

Evening. Granville to Stag. I filled stockings, iced cake etc. then waited for him to return and bring their new desks in from the garden hut. He only brought in Elizabeth's and pretended he didn't know there was only one!

No wonder he didn't want to go into toy dept. I've never felt so awful in all my life.

CHRISTMAS DAY

Awake wondering how to tell them there was only one desk and one chair. Granville saying the shop had made a mistake when I asked why hadn't he checked before? He must have cancelled one, not able to pay for two, without telling me.

In the middle of the night I had a brainwave. In block letters, a pencil message from Father Christmas. So sorry, he had sat on one of the chairs and it broke. Rudolf his reindeer had tripped and broken the desk. But he would send another when the shops opened. 'Lots of Love, Father Christmas xxxx.'

G. – the horrible rat – stayed in bed all morning. Mother and Syd came in afternoon. Granville to Stag. I've never, never, had such an awful time.

BOXING DAY
Again I had all the work to do. He stayed in bed all morning.

Afternoon. Auntie Annie came to tea and brought presents. I was ever so pleased with her present for Caroline especially. A lovely deck chair for Teddy Bear or a doll. It delighted Caroline, and I felt that it made up for her Christmas Day disappointment. Although she still wrings my heart when she trots up to me and says, 'He promised though, didn't he?'

Evening. Granville to Stag. I talked with Annie. She agrees it was an awful thing to do to a child.

TUESDAY 27 DECEMBER
Both fireplaces to clean out again while G. stayed in bed. Loads of work to see to and felt if I went to his mother's with them and we weren't speaking there may be a scene – so stayed at home.

Evening. Granville to Stag again. I started writing a play.

WEDNESDAY 28 DECEMBER
12.30 p.m. Petrol bus to mother's. With Elizabeth and Caroline for dinner.

Afternoon. Knitting and watching *Wednesday Magazine* on their television. Cried when it showed Father Christmas bringing toys to children – I thought of Caroline and her missing desk.

Evening. Granville to doctor's then to Stag. I watched *Mother Goose* with Elizabeth and Caroline then played records for them when they were in bed.

THURSDAY 29 DECEMBER
Another letter from Midland Bank about Granville's non-payment of personal loans. Terribly upset when Granville still didn't explain what financial affairs are like. Threw pepper pot at him, but it missed and some went in Caroline's eyes. Made me feel worse. Why the blazes doesn't he talk and stop all these scenes?

Evening. He went to Stag. I ironed.

FRIDAY 30 DECEMBER
Granville stayed at work for dinner. Long walk with Elizabeth and Caroline. Before Granville went to Stag the doctor came to have a talk with him. He says if he doesn't begin discussing his financial affairs and giving me proper housekeeping money his affairs will have to be administrated for him.

NEW YEAR'S EVE
Took E. and C. to dancing class. Granville went shopping by himself, me alone also.

Afternoon. To mother's New Year's Eve party with Granville, E. and C., Shirley, Audrey, Mrs Cudworth, Annie, Philip, Uncle Willie and Marie there. Home in a

Elizabeth and Caroline. Photo reproduced in *Family Doctor* magazine. 1960.

taxi. Marriage hopeless this year. Elizabeth and Caroline grand. G. to Stag later. I knitted a doll's dress. When I said we needed new bedding, Granville merely said, 'Oh don't natter me.'

Morale of this story: if you don't want to be driven completely crackers, never get involved with moneylenders. Even worth joining a nudist colony before that if you hanker after new clothes!

1964

An Awful Time

CHRISTMAS EVE

Last shopping in town with Elizabeth and Caroline.

Afternoon. Preparations for tonight, when we are giving a pantomime across at Oaklands Home for Elderly. Only the lane to cross opposite, so doesn't matter if it snows. Mother came first and tidied front room. George next at 6.30 p.m. while mother was making E. and C. up for concert. Frank, Kathleen, Mavis, Alfred, Lynne and Joyce arrived. They gave *Cinderella* across at the old folks' home and sang carols. I came back before it was over to prepare supper.

Party in front room. All enjoyed ourselves. Frank took mother home in his car at 1 a.m. She was worried that Syd would be annoyed. When he came back said mother was throwing pebbles at the bedroom window. Didn't know if she got in or not. Kathleen, Frank, Granville and I drank sherry. I packed presents when they went.

CHRISTMAS DAY

Annie arrived first, then mother and Syd, obviously in a mood. Doris and Kathleen Driver came for tea. It transpired that Syd had locked mother out last night, and she'd been out in the cold for half an hour. After tea Caroline rubbed her hand on a chair after eating a toffee. Annie got on about when she put a piece of chewing gum on a chair when we went there for tea. Caroline went upstairs crying. I said I was fed up with this kind of Christmas Day. Syd bounced back off home in a temper. Previously, Granville had admitted he'd bought a goose instead of a turkey. None of us liked it. All in tears, and mother, Doris and Annie had a taxi at 11 p.m. instead of 12.30 p.m.

An *awful* time. I asked if anyone would like baked beans on toast if they were still hungry after they went.

WHATEVER THE LEAVES DO TELL YOU
MAY ONLY THE BEST COME TRUE!

A Christmas postcard
from Hazel's
collection (IV).

But Caroline delighted with her riding hat and riding coat. Elizabeth not as keen on being astride a horse. Preferred some games. Also bought a riding whip, but not for use. Just to complete the picture!

BOXING DAY
All worn out after yesterday. Not up till midday. Tidied living room.

Evening. To pantomime in town with Elizabeth, Caroline, mother and Syd. Had been snowing. A drunk passed Caroline, pressed 2*s* into her hand and said, 'Buy yourself a Scotch'.

SUNDAY 27 DECEMBER
Up late again. To mother's. Doris and Annie too, and we were all on our friendliest behaviour! Home in taxi at midnight.

MONDAY 28 DECEMBER
Stayed in all day. Tidied front room. Knitted. An almighty relief not to have any plans. Granville washed and ironed. We all watched a play in the evening in front room.

TUESDAY 29 DECEMBER
Granville back to work. Gupta telephoned. Miss Mayall telephoned to ask if I'd like to take E. and C. for tea, but too busy. Earlier Kathleen had 'phoned to ask me to take a suitcase for some clothes a friend of hers had given her for me (*never* thought I'd be on the receiving end of charity – but kind of her).

Evening. Granville to Pack Horse working. Back in the old routine.

WEDNESDAY 30 DECEMBER
Up late. On 2.35 bus to Kathleen's at Kirkburton with Elizabeth and Caroline, who wore her new riding mac, red boots and scarlet 'horse' patterned headscarf. Tried lots of clothes on. Home 5 p.m. Tea. Granville stayed in.

NEW YEAR'S EVE
Morning. Cleaning living room and hall while E. and C. were still in bed. Got them up at 10.30 a.m. Went up lane to ask Mrs Broadbent if she will come for tea tomorrow, then to Joyce's but she was out. Shopping at Moldgreen. On 1.45 bus to Outlane Farm (Whittaker's). I stayed in the house with the riding school proprietor's three small boys while Elizabeth and Caroline went for a ride on Shrimp and Dinah. [Those small boys, especially John Whittaker, became famous show riders.]

Town. More shopping. Home for tea. Granville to Pack Horse. I washed their yellow riding pullovers etc. TV, knitting. Reading *Yorkshire Evening Post*. A good ending to 1964. I have an 'It Happened to Me' letter to finish the year with.

Joyce telephoned to say she can come tomorrow E. and C. still awake, as usual, at midnight. Fed up with the way they carry on.

1967

Near Collapse

MONDAY 11 DECEMBER

Helped Caroline down slippery lane as she had violin as well as her satchel to carry. Rolled lots of *Examiner*s into firelighters. Town with Elizabeth. Bought a few Christmas cards. Even they are very expensive to what they used to be. A really good one is over a shilling. This evening Granville working at the Lion pub.

WEDNESDAY 13 DECEMBER

Breathed a sigh of relief when Elizabeth returned to school and the house free of arguments for a few hours. Repair man came from Whitfields to take wireless. Said the transistorised ones are always requiring more attention. So much for progress.

Evening. Annual General Meeting Huddersfield Authors' Circle. George afterwards for coffee with Pat, Joyce Woodhouse and Dorothy.

SATURDAY 16 DECEMBER

To doctor with Caroline. She has German measles, and he has given me some white medicine for the nerves of my stomach.

Afternoon. Shopping in town with Caroline and Elizabeth. Granville brought wireless back from repair.

Evening. He went to the Lion as usual. Nasty as anything when he came back. Smelt foul. He knows that Christmas is almost here and we are in the usual financial Queer Street. I can't buy all that needs to be bought without money. Elizabeth crying the other night saying aren't we having *any* decorations or a tree? He said that the hall would definitely be decorated for Christmas. (What with, unpaid bills?) Now he knows it's all been talk and doesn't know what to do. I was so angry I slept with Elizabeth.

MONDAY 18 DECEMBER

Sunny and bright but white frost on rooftops. Feeling very poorly. Tight pains across my stomach, sickly, wanting to double up. Caroline couldn't find her shoes. As usual, I got the brunt of it when they turned up beneath table in front room. Xmas shopping in town. Miserable with no money. Caroline home for dinner and to change into purple velvet party dress, purple and white spotted hair ribbons, white knee-length socks. Greenhead School party. Granville met her at 6.30 p.m. He had to take her to a toilet before coming home because she said she'd been waiting for a long time, and couldn't go at the party because they might start a game while she was out. Elizabeth to Youth Orchestra. Granville to Lion.

TUESDAY 19 DECEMBER

Cleaning, supermarket at Waterloo.

Evening. Granville to Lion. Ironed. Very frosty and cold night. When he came back said the landlord says he needn't go again until Saturday night, but has to work all the Christmas evenings.

WEDNESDAY 20 DECEMBER

Bright frosty day. Ordered a green travelling case for Elizabeth's 'big' present. (For when she goes to Paris with her school.) A detective game for Caroline (29s 6d). I'm finding presents more difficult to choose now they are past the 'pram and doll' stage.

Lovely surprise when I returned home – after borrowing £2 more of Elizabeth and Caroline's – to receive a five-guinea cheque for this week's best letter in *Tit-Bits*.

THURSDAY 21 DECEMBER

Milder. So white toppings on rooftops and grass, and no windows to go round mopping condensation up from sills. Wrote Christmas cards in front bedroom, still feeling weak and sometimes sick.

Afternoon. Shopping in town after changing five-guinea cheque. Spent £4 of it on presents and food. Met Caroline from Greenhead. Evening. Granville to Lion. I read Caroline's first Greenhead High School magazine.

FRIDAY 22 DECEMBER

Felt exceptionally ill after they had gone to school. Doubled up with pains in stomach, backache and headache. Legs feeling weak as anything. But had to force myself to do work required for Christmas. Made almond paste for cakes. Cleaned outside living room, kitchen and front room windows. Feeling like death all the time. Vacced, polished furniture. In a state of near collapse when Granville returned from work.

Evening. Elizabeth, Caroline and Sarah Venables went carol singing up the lane. Granville stayed in as I went to bed earlier than usual feeling so ill.

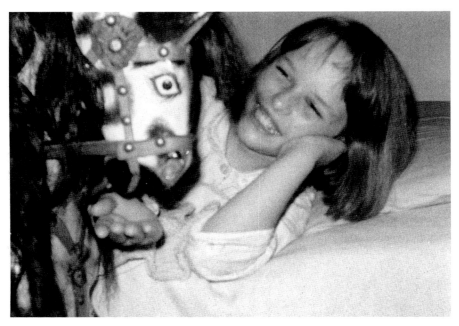

Caroline and Lilac Domino, her rocking horse. Christmas 1967.

SATURDAY 23 DECEMBER
Shopping all day in town with Elizabeth and Caroline. Whitfields midday. Still don't feel like eating anything. Feel sick at thought of food. So I wouldn't feel 'out of place' if going out at Christmas I bought (on account, at Kaye's) a cream-coloured fur fabric coat for £10 19s 6d, and a red cardigan. Fur fabric anorak for Caroline and red trews.

CHRISTMAS EVE
Afternoon. To mother's for tea. Bus to town 11.15 p.m. A lot of drunken hooligans and awful people rolling around. Elizabeth was frightened – glad to get into the safety of the parish church for the midnight service. Elizabeth cried at one part, but Caroline and I were laughing. Out of the silence suddenly came two loud and uncouth belches. And a man opposite kept puffing his lips out. We walked home, nearly two miles. I then wrapped presents and filled stockings. Granville at the Lion.

CHRISTMAS DAY
Rainy morning. Very mild for December. Opening presents in front room. Mother and Syd came in the afternoon for tea. Mother and I went across to Oaklands to give the old ladies some different faces to see. Syd, Elizabeth and Caroline played new games. They left in a taxi at 9.45 p.m.

Christmas 1967 with friends from the Authors' Circle. Left to right: Caroline, Nora Hennigan, Ellen Mayall, Ivy Broadbent, Elizabeth, Miss Sayles. 1967.

THURSDAY 28 DECEMBER
Trying to rest and get better. Doing a few trade competitions. Elizabeth to supermarket. Don't feel like eating anything yet.

FRIDAY 29 DECEMBER
To doctor's with Caroline. He says the infection, which is spreading, takes about three weeks to incubate. That's why I've been feeling so awful. To chemist and supermarket. Elizabeth stayed in bed reading her new book, called *Fifteen*. Washed and ironed. To Dorothy and Joe Crawshaw's for tea. Joe's sister and brother-in-law there. Granville came from work.

SATURDAY 30 DECEMBER
Shopping in town with E., C. and Granville. Syd had 'elevenses' with us in Whitfields. Cooked dinner for Elizabeth and Caroline. Granville and I didn't have any. He went to the Lion tonight. We three stayed in. I knitted. Watched TV.

NEW YEAR'S EVE
Preparing for party. Ellen Mayall, Miss Sayles (Authors' Circle) and Mrs Broadbent and Nora (nurse), both from up Greenhead Lane, for the evening. Lots couldn't come because of sudden snow and icy roads this morning.

Miss Taylor, music teacher, couldn't come because she has a cold. Granville walked up after midnight with Mrs Broadbent to her cottage so he would be the first dark-haired man to 'let in' the New Year for her. Lucky if the first person has dark hair. We have a dark-haired man permanently in our house, so why aren't we lucky all year round?

1969
As Though I Was Choking

SUNDAY 21 DECEMBER

Woke early. Terrified with my loss of voice. Asked Granville to get Mrs Venables. But she didn't get up for hours. Felt as though I was choking. Granville then went to Beech Avenue to see if Dr Selbie could tell him anywhere to have a prescription prepared. Came back and telephoned an Almondbury chemist who said he would attend to him. Even then they hadn't the correct lozenges and sent a substitute. Voice went fainter all day.

Afternoon. Mother came, had tea here. Granville, mother, Elizabeth and Caroline to candlelight carol service at Dalton St Paul's. I had to stay at home. Did the ironing and tried to say 'Merry Christmas' out loud to see if my voice would work.

MONDAY 22 DECEMBER

Still can't talk properly. Wrapped orange rug, Harvey's Bristol Cream sherry, small Brontë Liqueur, and the white and green beret I'd knitted for mother. E. & C. took them up fields then went to town with her. They had tea in town then mother called here to see how I am. Mrs Broadbent called, and went back with mother for the evening.

TUESDAY 23 DECEMBER

Elizabeth to coffee morning at a Bradley teacher's.

Afternoon. Elizabeth to supermarket with Caroline then took mince pies for mother. I did some washing.

Evening. E. and C. to Bible study at Lloyd Mellor's. Mrs Wheeler telephoned to say Margaret is poorly so we can't go for Christmas Day. Thought it was too good to be true, not having to spend the day cooking. She is not to be relied upon at all. Yet I always have to soldier on, even with no voice. Mrs Broadbent here for evening. Says mother can go to her house on Christmas Day.

CHRISTMAS EVE
Mild, drizzly morning. Granville now having to do extra shopping for vegetables etc. in town. Then to mother's. Telephoned to say her foot is bad and she won't go to Mrs Broadbent's. Feels like a pack of cards collapsing down.

Afternoon. Granville and I shopping in town. Elizabeth to town by herself. Caroline stayed in.

Evening. Stayed in by myself. Granville to Crescent. E. and C. with Youth Fellowship carolling. Back at 1.30 a.m.

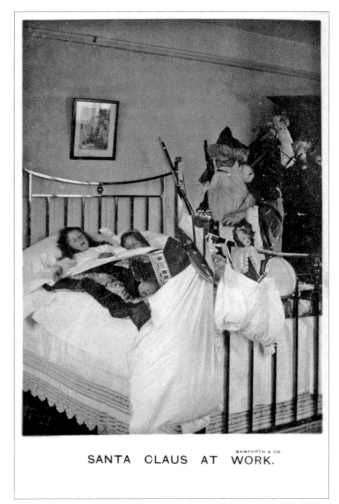

SANTA CLAUS AT WORK.

A Christmas postcard from Hazel's collection (V).

I polished furniture and washed shelves. Watched *The Merry Widow* on TV. Might as well be one myself. Dorothy Crawshaw from Authors' Circle at mother's. Raining.

CHRISTMAS DAY

Problem of mother solved – arrived by car. People who live at Fernside picked her up as she was walking down. After looking at E. and C.'s presents upstairs she went to Mrs Broadbents for Xmas dinner and tea. They called here after 10 p.m. when Fiona and her husband had left. Mother stayed night at Mrs B.'s.

We had turkey for tea and vegetables. Turkey donated to Granville by Crescent landlord. Watched TV and read.

BOXING DAY

Mother came down about 11 a.m. Awful her being a widow for the second time since Syd died in January. Granville went to ask Leonard Hoyle if he'd like to come here. He will be alone. He jumped at the chance! We all had sandwiches etc. and coffee then mother, E. and C. went up the fields to the flat first. Granville and I took Leonard for a walk in the park. Mother's for tea. Miss Hirst, never been married – neither has Leonard – there too. Stayed talking till 12.45 a.m. Leonard was Syd's brother-in-law.

No need for anybody to be alone, really. If others are, ask them. They don't ask for posh meals – just to be included, and for laughter and a bit of companionship. Leonard has never been married, so no family of his own either.

SATURDAY 27 DECEMBER

Supermarket. Frost all day.

Afternoon. Ironing. Elizabeth in bed, headache. Caroline and I up fields to mother's. Gathering wood for fire down fields afterwards. Granville took presents for Annie. After tea he went to Crescent. I re-typed a story. Knitted. At 11.15 p.m. Granville returned – he had been given a lift in a car driven by a new barmaid. He always told me they only had waiters. He brought her in and when she took her fur coat off I was furious. She wore a pink shiny dress, exceedingly low cut, and her huge chest was exposed. High-heeled 'gold' shoes and a vivid pink chiffon scarf round her shoulders. I had just had a wash, no make-up on, old jumper and skirt, slippers, and my hair all twiddled.

I made coffee, but as I poured it stood on Granville's foot and glared at him. Both smelled of drink. I slept with Elizabeth.

SUNDAY 28 DECEMBER

Granville stayed in Elizabeth's bed till 1 p.m. When he came down I told him to telephone the Crescent and say he wasn't going anymore. He said no one would be there. So I telephoned. Of course they were in.

DATE	AMOUNT OF POUNDS IN WORDS				PAY TO THE ORDER OF	CHEQUE AMOUNT	DISCOUNT	CHEQUE N
	THOUSANDS	HUNDREDS	TENS	UNITS				
69 MAY 30				----ONE--	MRS. HAZEL WHEELER	1. 10. 0		3,309.

HUDDERSFIELD EXAMINER
EXAMINER OFFICE, RAMSDEN STREET, HUDDERSFIELD
REMITTANCE ADVICE

Nº 003309

SHILLINGS AND PENCE AS FIGURES

HEREWITH OUR CHEQUE IN SETTLEMENT OF YOUR ACCOUNT.
Yours faithfully,

JOSEPH WOODHEAD & SONS LTD.

Payment for a contribution to the *Huddersfield Examiner*, 30 May 1969.

Afternoon. Mother, Miss Hirst and Doris here for tea. Elizabeth to Susan Johnson's. Caroline to chapel and Youth Fellowship.

MONDAY 29 DECEMBER
Snowing. Caroline and I shopping in town. Bought her a scarlet dress from C&A for tomorrow evening's party at chapel. They went to Bible study.

NEW YEAR'S EVE
Caroline and I up fields to see mother. Gathered load of wood for fire on way down. We all then enjoyed watching Elizabeth Taylor in *National Velvet* on television.
Evening. Granville and Elizabeth up fields by torchlight to see mother. Miss Hirst was there.

[Most of my writing earnings from *Huddersfield Examiner* listed at back of diary.]

The Best Christmas Ever

Mother had not been to Boroughbridge – where she was born – for many years, so I thought it would be a wonderful Christmas if she was taken there. Especially as she was a widow for the second time. Who can enjoy Christmas if someone else is sad and lonely?

So I wrote to the Yorkshire Post *asking, 'Does anyone remember Hilda?' and sent a photograph of her when aged fourteen and a milliner's apprentice there. Her dad was the village policeman, and they lived in New Row, next to the police station. How thrilled she'd have been had she lived long enough to see her picture on the front of the book I wrote about the Haigh family.*

Letters galore came. School friends of many decades ago all clamouring for us to take Hilda to stay at the Crown Hotel for Christmas! I could hardly wait to meet them, having heard about those – until now – shadowy figures from the past...

FRIDAY 17 DECEMBER
A fine day. Mild for time of year.

9.40 a.m. With Caroline to have a corn removed. It cost 60p. Bought purple blouse for her, £2. Sandwiches and coffee in Whitfields. More shopping. Bought brown purse for Annie, 45p from Kayes. A big place mat with old-fashioned picture called 'The Return Home' to give to Ethel Hope on Christmas Day. Called at Mrs Broadbent's. Mother there for the weekend.

Evening. Uncle Willie telephoned to thank me for copy of *Yorkshire Life*. Caroline to a party. Elizabeth working at library till 8.30 p.m. then to Starlight dancing. With Julie. Granville out with men from work. I typed an article.

SATURDAY 18 DECEMBER
Granville serving hot dogs at football match. Here's his account of it:

> Came at 1 p.m. Collected my pass to get into the ground. 'Tell 'em it's a new one,' chap said.
>
> Saw the chap again. 'Right, it's all set up outside under the score board. All you need is this can of hot water and that's it.'
>
> Filled the trays and lit the gas. First the onions, which take longest to get ready, then the sausages and beefburgers. A queue in no time and trying to put the sausage between the bread with gale blowing and trying to put the onions over the lot.
>
> Then drama! Had 500 pieces of paper to wrap the goods in. Took one, wind came and blew the lot all over the Terrace Side. So from then on no paper to wrap up the goods. But the band was playing, Christmas spirit in the crowds – when all sold out the accounting for all that was left.
>
> 'How is it you have six beefburgers left and no bread? When you set off there was just enough bread for each burger and sausage.'
>
> 'Ha ha, and what about those dropped on the floor with my cold hands?'
>
> 'Oh you aren't supposed to waste any, profits going...'
>
> 'Profit me foot, if they drop they drop and that's it,' I told him.
>
> 'Oh, OK – anyway, well done, you have sold double the amount we usually sell – will you come next match?'
>
> After smelling coat sleeve and cap, both smelling like a hot dog.
>
> It were good fun, and a bit extra for taking grandma to Boroughbridge for Christmas. Granville Wheeler.

SUNDAY 19 DECEMBER
My left eye very red and bloodshot. The colour of Christmas. Upsetting.

Made Cornish pasties for early lunch. Elizabeth teaching at Sunday School. Granville painting living room primrose yellow. Anticipating spring.

Afternoon. Watched *David Copperfield* on TV. Salmon sandwiches, fresh fruit salad, cake for tea.

Evening. Carol service by candlelight at Dalton St Paul's with mother, Mrs Broadbent and Granville.

MONDAY 20 DECEMBER
To Dr Grayson. He tested my eye. Had to pay 40p for drops and ointment.

Afternoon. Shopping in town. Bought another heavy tin of paint, 45p, red tablecloth and four serviettes on account at Kaye's, £1.85. To use tomorrow when Frank Foster (mother's childhood schoolfriend who saw the article in the *Yorkshire Post*) comes for tea.

Evening. Mrs Foster telephoned to say Frank can't come tomorrow. In bed with bronchitis.

Caroline, Granville, Hilda and
Elizabeth in Boroughbridge, 1971.

THURSDAY 23 DECEMBER

Mild, sunny. Washing. To town with Caroline after coffee and Christmas cake and cheese. So busy in town we didn't bother about any lunch. Bought a net Christmas stocking, chocolate mouse, purse etc. to fill stocking at Boroughbridge for mother. Early tea with Caroline.

Evening. To supermarket with her. Absolutely packed out. Couldn't get up some aisles at all.

Granville out with men from work. Elizabeth singing at Storthes Hall (the old 'lunatic asylum'). Then to CSSM party.

Ironed after coming back from supermarket. Caroline revising. Wrapped present to take to Boroughbridge. Looking forward to Christmas this year.

CHRISTMAS EVE

Preparing to go to Boroughbridge for Christmas. Elizabeth working at library till 5 p.m. Mother here early. We had some tea about 3.15 p.m. She telephoned Frank Foster – first time she's heard his voice since they were children. His dad was a policeman too, living next door to the Haighs.

Taxi arrived at 5 p.m. We picked Elizabeth up in town. Arrived at Crown Hotel 6.30 p.m. after a trouble-free ride. Mother had a single bedroom, no. 28. Our double bedrooms were nos 14 and 12. That made me feel mean. Mother the only one alone. Wonderful Yorkshire welcome from staff at the Crown Hotel! Unlit rural dark streets. Called first to see R. Wilson, antiques dealer. He had been ill with bronchitis so didn't stay long. Then invited into a Mr and Mrs Kitchen's house. He was with mother's brother Ernie when he was killed in the First World War.

Next on the list of the many who wanted to be reunited with mother was Emily Robinson. Granville rang the doorbell. After all the intervening years of silence mother was a bit apprehensive about how to introduce herself. The cottage door opened. A little bit of a nervous cough from mother – 'Oh, er, I'm the late Hilda Haigh...'

Emily must have thought a true life ghost of Christmas Past stood hovering on her doorstep. No need for any ice breaking after such an introduction on a black dark Christmas Eve!

The place erupted with uncontrollable laughter. Which continued through a magical, nostalgic evening of warm mince pies, cheese, Christmas cake – homemade, naturally – and do-you-remembers?

'Second childhood.' Hilda on swing in Boroughbridge, Christmas 1971.

Emily's parents in their eighties, delighted to have 'one of their own' back among them. Back to the Crown for a drink before Midnight service at St James' Church, which mother used to attend when a girl.

Nothing better than old friends, especially at Christmas! Sheer delight on the faces of all, at greeting 'the late Hilda Haigh' again on Christmas Eve. Far better than Marley's ghost! We could have gone on talking and greeting with no feeling of tiredness, so much so that when we returned to the Crown Hotel on Christmas morning at around 1 a.m. the doors were locked!

The policeman who we spoke to when calling at the old police station earlier happened to be walking by – he knocked very loudly the big black knocker, and the wandering flock was welcomed into the 'home from home' of the Crown Hotel. How delighted I felt that mother was not alone to greet the Christmas morn!

We tucked mother into the cosy bed and warned her that Father Christmas might come, so go to sleep, night-night, see you in the morning.

CHRISTMAS DAY

We all grouped round mother as she opened her stocking, as she did all those years ago, when her sister Ella cracked Hilda's head on the brass knob of the bed, because she had a white mouse and mother's was pink. Necessitating Grandad Haigh (as he was to become) cutting the sugar mice in half. Therefore each getting a top half and a bottom half with a curly tail.

Then we left her to get dressed. She was so excited and delighted at the prospect of having breakfast not alone, she came into the dining room wearing, besides a smile that would have lit a thousand candles, her new scarlet jumper on back-to-front. Inside-out as well.

This only added to the joviality of that best of all Christmas mornings. After a superb breakfast served by the most pleasant of staff, and surrounded by mistletoe and holly and a huge decorated tree, all seated at a round table, we went for a walk in the sunshine.

Took photographs of mother outside the vicarage where she used to attend the Girls' Friendly Society, and on a swing, and swooping down a helter-skelter. Then to visit the cemetery where Grandma and Grandad Haigh, and Ernie's war grave, are. After a drink in the Black Bull, back to the Crown for lunch. All voting it the best Christmas ever, no matter what disasters future ones may bring! Then to renew acquaintance with Ethel Hope and her husband Ernest in their bungalow.

Talking, hardly time for tea for 'telling tales of long ago', but it was delicious – talking till almost 11 p.m., then back to the Crown.

BOXING DAY

A sunny, white frost. A perfect day. Walked to Aldborough with Granville. Mother, Elizabeth and Caroline in Ethel's car to visit old school friend Kathleen Slack (née Mortis). Warmest of welcomes. How much more Christmassy a cottage in the

'Let me in!' Prince in 1966.

country is than a posh London hotel! A fire in the hearth, a kettle on the hob, refreshments. Oh that Eternity could be something like that! Called at another schoolfriend's – Marjorie Foster. Then Ethel and Ernest took us to the Three Horseshoes for lunch before going back to their bungalow for more conversation and tea round the fire.

Elizabeth and Caroline to a church service before having a final farewell drink at the Crown Hotel. Taxi came for us at 9.30 p.m. Patches of fog on return journey. Mother taken to her flat first. Prince excited to see us back. A neighbour had looked after her.

Under the Tree

Christmas crackers nowadays are expensive and frequently disappointing. But having bought an Army & Navy Stores circular from 1929 it's wonderful to relive that Christmas by browsing through the pages.

A Tom Smith's 6s box of crackers, decorated with jesters and pierrots, contained a pierrot hat and frill, comical noses, musical toys, and quips and jokes.

A 'Monster Box', twenty inches long, tied with silk ribbon, in orange, green or red, cost 32s. Each cracker containing six articles, pretty fans, miniature bottles of perfume, jewellery, curios, headdresses, novelties, and 'up to date' proverbs.

5s 9d could buy a box of brilliant green and crimson gelatine crackers containing artistic headdresses, fireworks, fire balloons, and magic messages.

Mead & Field's Crackers were a 4s box of scarlet crackers with frilled ends, containing miniature footballs, a greyhound game, berets etc.

Remember Sparagnapane's Crackers? A box of six cost 9s. Brilliant crimson, decorated with crimson muslin fans and crimson and silver dragonflies. Containing curios, perfumes and jewels, with head-dresses and love verses.

Caley's Crackers had a splendid variety. Some contained golf hats, clubs and other novelties – all for 2s 8d. A 5s 6d box was decorated with cone sprays, cap and with a parlour game in each. The 3s 6d version held balloons, puffballs, and flying sausages.

One set had musical toys inside for only 1s 1d a box. The lid portrayed a curious black cat listening to a gramophone.

Mansell Hunt's Crackers, 3s 6d a box, contained tossballs, beauty patches, turf games, hats and caps. The Army & Navy Drapery Department that Christmas of 1929 had the ever-popular gift of gloves in abundance. Ladies Natural Musquash Gauntlet, lined with rabbit fur throughout, 60s. Beaver Coney Gauntlet lined with

Sparagnapane's Crackers

AC T130—These seasonable Crackers are made in red and brown and decorated with sprays of holly and robins ; they contain an excellent selection of head-dresses and love verses .. per box of **6 5/-**

AC 621—Tango and orange crepe, gold flittered with Father Christmas centres ; each cracker contains a hat or cap and a novelty .. .. per box **8/3**

AC T166—Attractive Crackers in pale orange crepe with gold flittered frilled ends, decorated with Thé Roses to tone ; they contain a selection of jewels, together with hats and caps .. per box of **6 9/9**

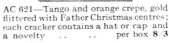

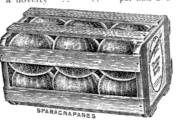

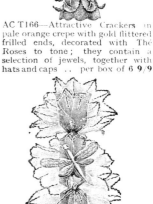

AC T105—Effective scarlet crepe Crackers, decorated with mistletoe sprays ; they contain a selection of head-dresses and love verses.
Per box of **6 5/-**

AC 1029—A good model of a wooden crate of oranges. The 12 realistic card oranges each contain a novelty, hat or cap and a snap .. per crate **3/6**

AC T160—Brilliant crimson Crackers decorated with crimson muslin fans and crimson and silver dragon-flies ; they contain curios, perfumes and jewels together with head-dresses and love verses. Per box of **6 9/-**

AC 571—Red crepe Crackers with fancy ends and Santa Claus reliefs ; they contain a variety of hats and caps .. .. per box **3/6**

AC 585—Popular Crackers with tango crepe ends and gold embossed centres with pictures of humorous bandsmen ; they contain musical toys and head-dresses in each cracker .. .. .. per box **4/-**

Advertisement for Sparagnapane's Crackers, Christmas 1929.

wool, 30s 6d. In language so different to that of modern times, 'Useful sweater in Gay Colours' – 45s. Another, 'For the Matron [age-wise, not a person working in a hospital] in nigger/champagne and other shades' – 45s.

Fancy garters were amusing gifts, in pretty pale shades. Trimmed with flowers or imitation jewels, 6s 11d. Or how about a boudoir cap of beige lace, trimmed with ribbons in three tones, for 7s 11d?

Long before wearing trousers for small girls became a way of life, I remember wearing gaiters as a child of two in 1929 – and the time it took to fasten all the buttons up each leg.

Gaiters are advertised in the catalogue as serviceable Christmas gifts. A pair of Fox's Overknee Stockinette ones for ladies cost from 9s 9d to 12s 11d then.

'Tasteful Novelties in Fancy Linens' were often given as presents. Attractively boxed breakfast sets, consisting of a tray cloth, a 'Good Morning!' cosy cover, an egg cosy cover and a serviette. In fine Irish linen, appliquéd in contrasting colours.

Before smoking was known to be harmful, anything to do with that was a good old standby gift for gentlemen. Silver-plated cigarette box, a tobacco jar with a modern figure as a pipe rest, Havana cigars, Cabanas, Rothschilds, in boxes of twenty-five, cost 108s for 100.

In those wonderful years when people wrote letters in real pen and ink, one might have been given an inkstand with a nickel and enamel finish, 7s 9d. Or a blotter in nickel and enamel, 5s 9d from the Army & Navy catalogue.

Turning pages of an old Christmas catalogue is like being a time traveller in a time when to be given a Parker fountain pen and matching pencil was to have attained the height of sophistication. Especially if another gift happened to be a smart box of stationery. When this happened, I could hardly wait to begin writing a thank you letter on eight pages of thick, 'posh' notepaper. The box was useful for housing, maybe, jewellery or love letters. I still have, in this twenty-first century, a small box of 'gold' pen nibs. How some things pass into the mists of time! Hardly ever seen now are pencil sharpeners and erasers.

How romantic gentlemen looked, wearing white silk scarves for evening wear. They could be bought for 35s, 37s 6d or 45s from the Army & Navy Store back in 1929. Another favourite with gentlemen was a pure wool scarf in natural camel shade, 7s 5d, 8s 5d, or 10s 6d. Men wore fur-backed gloves, too. One of the most expensive pairs was made from real opossum with cape palms and lined with lambswood, at 125s. It is rare to see men wearing any type of gloves at all today – they prefer to sloppily hide their hands beneath overlong sleeves.

Never losing their appeal are toilet soap and perfume gift sets. Exactly right for popping into a 1929 Christmas stocking are a delightful set of bottle of perfume and two tablets of soap. In lavender, violet, or Eau de Cologne, at 2s 6d – half a crown – each. You punctuated the hours by sniffing them and dipping into chocolate boxes. Savouring joys to come.

Does anyone recall Atkinson's Californian Poppy, a box of three tablets for 2s 9d, and Lilac and Lilies for 3s 9d? Or Field's Spermaceti, White Rose, and 'Our Nell'?

Today, some collect biscuit tins from the 1920s. All manner of novelty shapes were produced, including Crawford's Motor Bus, 2s 4d. A big tin of biscuits was a good present for a family – something to eat was always welcome.

Then there were those novelties with cotton wool masquerading as snow. Joy bombs, which exploded with small gifts. We had a snowman that was brought out Christmas after Christmas, and filled with new novelties. Also a Gipsy Caravan. And 10s gift boxes containing eight drawers, each filled with superb chocolates or sweets. Individually wrapped, looking too good to eat. Fondants, sugared almonds, heavenly shades of mauve, palest pink pralines, nougat, Turkish delight, crystallised fruits, orange and lemon slices. I kept the papers, shiny and colourful, and rolled them into a ball for Pussy to play with later.

Gone, but never forgotten by those who woke on Christmas mornings in the 1920s and '30s were the compendiums of games, conjuring outfits, blow football, jazz band sets and Meccano outfits lying on the bed alongside the stocking filled with smaller gifts.

Such joys advertised in the Army & Navy Catalogue as 'All Reliable British Made Toys': china dolls, tea sets, doll houses, bus conductor sets.

Setting the festive scene for all those delights was the Christmas tree. In 1929 a big five-foot one from the Army & Navy Stores cost 6s 6d. Turkeys and geese could only be trussed for town orders received prior to Saturday 21 December. Instructions had to be given when ordering, the charge being 1s per bird.

A Box Brownie camera in 1929, perfect for capturing those festive moments, cost from 10s 6d to 25s. Musical entertainment was largely do-it-yourself in those days. A ukulele may be bought for 6s, but a genuine Hawaiian model in a case cost anything from 32s 6d to £3 15s. Other popular musical instruments were concertinas, banjos and accordions. Not forgetting carol singing around the piano.

How sterile our modern Christmases are for those old enough to remember – if only slightly – those marvellous Christmases of yesteryear. It's crackers, when you think about it, swapping those for the TV-dominated festivities of the twenty-first century.

1974

An Awful Smell

WEDNESDAY 4 DECEMBER

Bus to Aspley. Mildred Coldwell and Irene Brook (the builder's wife) met me. In Irene's car to literary luncheon at Kershaw House with *Yorkshire Ridings Magazine*. Speakers Leslie Thomas and Monica Dickens, Charles Dickens' granddaughter. Spoke to both and obtained photographs.

Editor Winston Halstead asked us to chat with Leslie Thomas for a photograph to be put in the magazine. Speaking to Charles Dickens' granddaughter prior to Christmas!

Enjoyable meal. Heavy rain on way home. Elizabeth's day off from library. Whopping big fly got in when I opened a window and we spent half an hour chasing it and being chased. It was like a big black bomber. Stayed in and watched TV.

Elizabeth to West Riding pub in town. Earning extra for Christmas.

THURSDAY 5 DECEMBER

In the evening to last Greenhead High School Speech Day. Sat in gallery of Huddersfield Town Hall with Granville. Glad Caroline finished before it became a sixth form college. It seemed out of place to have big hefty lads with long hair – some even with moustaches, and one or two coloured ones – as pupils of Greenhead High School for Girls. As it was in my time there.

Wouldn't want Caroline to be going there now. Headmaster Mr Cookson, however, is an improvement on Miss Owen. He looked very attractive with his black hair and black gown lined with scarlet across the shoulder. Contrasting with the green-topped platform table and front, massed with huge scarlet Christmas roses. Excited when Caroline walked on stage for her certificate. Only a couple of brief, uninteresting carols. How different to the occasions when Miss Spikes was music mistress.

> *The Yorkshire Ridings Magazine*
> *and*
> *The Square Bookshop, Heptonstall*
>
> *welcome you to the*
>
> ## *Ridings Literary Luncheon*
>
> *at Kershaw House, Luddenden, near Halifax, on*
>
> *Wednesday, December 4th, 1974*
>
> *11.30 a.m. for 12.30 p.m.*
>
> *Speakers: Monica Dickens and Leslie Thomas*
>
> *Ticket: £2.65 (including wine)*

Ticket for the Ridings Literary Luncheon at Kershaw House, 4 December 1974.

> GREENHEAD COLLEGE
>
> HUDDERSFIELD
>
> # SPEECH DAY
>
> Thursday, 5th December, 1974
>
> at 7 p.m.
> IN THE TOWN HALL
>
> **BALCONY**   Row   **4**   Seat **20**

Ticket for Greenhead College Speech Day in Huddersfield Town Hall, 5 December 1974.

CHRISTMAS DAY

A cyclone demolished Darwin in Australia today. Drizzling. Rushed up to Almondbury Church for 11.15 a.m. for carol service. Walked home. Salad, Christmas cake, cheese, coffee.

Afternoon. Opening presents. Jumpers I have bought for Elizabeth and Caroline were too big, so will have to get then something instead. Granville gave me a stone milk jug which I like, but he'll have to return tights which are awful. Black, with rows of holes up the sides and a hot water bottle in a cover. Which will get dingy, and I prefer to feel heat instead of diluted warmth.

Turkey, carrots, sprouts, potatoes and fresh fruit salad for tea.

Evening. No buses so Elizabeth walked to town to meet a boy she met last night. Caroline and Granville watched TV. I read *Vet in Harness*. Margaret 'phoned to say John wouldn't be coming tomorrow, and we had to ignore him.

9 p.m. John telephoned to ask if it would be alright if he did come. Think he wanted to go on a hunt, then realised it was on Friday, not Thursday.

BOXING DAY

Only thing I enjoyed today was listening to *The Shepherd's Farewell* on radio. I said I'd like it played at my funeral. Raining. Preparing for Annie Whitworth, Margaret, John and Grandma Wheeler. Put pudding on to steam. Made stuffing and mustard sauce. They arrived about twelve. Mrs Wheeler had her walking stick with her, which was ridiculous, taking loads of room up awkwardly in taxi. Later, when she went to toilet (in hallway on a chamber that Granville had bought at a jumble sale) there was an awful smell throughout the house. Felt quite sick. Granville, John and Bruno for usual walk. I was washing up then after being in front room for a while glad to get in kitchen again to prepare tea. They left in taxi at 8 p.m. Annie stayed till 9.40 p.m. We had supper and watched Danny La Rue. Elizabeth has been in a terrible mood today. Margaret said she had a wicked temper and Annie thinks she doesn't look well. Who would, after the jumble sale 'toilet' episode?

Glad it's over for another year.

FRIDAY 27 DECEMBER

Cleaned both fireplaces out, loads of washing. Evening with Granville on bus to infirmary to visit Bob Richardson. Frightening going into side ward where he was absolutely oblivious or our presence.

SATURDAY 28 DECEMBER

High winds. Paid £1 each for diaries for E. and C. They don't fill big ones in like I do.

Afternoon. Usual walk with Granville and Bruno. Gathered trolley full of wood for fires.

Evening. Reading *Vet in Harness*.

Granville at the top of Greenhead
Lane, December 1975.

SUNDAY 29 DECEMBER
Still windy.
    Afternoon. Walk with Granville and Bruno.
    Evening. By fire with Granville. Watching TV and drinking whisky and orange.

MONDAY 30 DECEMBER
Mild, dry day. Made all three beds, vacced living room. Washed woollies.
    Afternoon. Typing and writing article about expectant mothers in the 1920s. E.
and C. home for tea. Granville out with dominos team from work. Elizabeth out
with a boy called Douglas. Caroline and I watched a Charlie Chaplin silent film,
The Gold Rush.

NEW YEAR'S EVE
Fine, mild. 10.15 train to Leeds with Granville. After drawing £10 out of bank,
G. bought some 'K' shoes, £4.99 in a sale. Ironing board cover 98p. Lunch in
Schofields. Talking to two retired ladies at our table. Bought four plates 45p each,
six small ones 10p each. China cup and saucer 49p. Paid £14 off £21 (G. paid the
rest) for chest of drawers for E. and C. Bought pair of pants each for them, 35p
and 50p.

has his own special section in the Hospital – they are all men except me – mainly elderly ones I'm afraid! So they've put me in a little room of me own at the side of the ward, apart from the nurses I'm devoid of feminine company – still I sit in the day lounge with all the old men – and listen to all their ailments – the lucky lot!!

I shall have to make this short Hazel – I seem to have a lot of letters to write thanking people for their cards & good wishes. I will contact you when I get back home. T'il then Love from Jeanne

A letter from Jeanne Wood to Hazel, written shortly before Jeanne's death from bladder cancer. 'We had been friends since the 1940s.'

Home on 5.15 train. Caroline had bought black trousers from C&A and I had to spend ages trying to cut out the red tab from behind.

(For lunch in Schofields, tomato soup and rolls. Haddock, parsley sauce, French beans, chips. Praline ice cream and coffee. Always better when Granville is with me. Can't talk with strangers and eat at the same time. He doesn't mind, and eats faster in any case, so mouth free for talking.)

Love the cosiness of home and a blazing fire after a pleasant winter day out.

Goodbye 1974 – year of roaring inflation. Goodbye too, Jeanne – till we meet again. She never wanted to be fifty! Older than me, but now I'll end up older than her…

In a sealed envelope earlier in the year, one of Prince's cat hairs. Also departed in 1974. But the solitary hair is still there. Immortal. And still visible, if the envelope is opened. But won't, 'cos don't want to lose it.

Trying to Get Away from It All

WEDNESDAY 22 DECEMBER

On 9.40 train to Leeds with Caroline. Waited till 11 a.m. for coach. Rough lot of people boarded it – all going to work at Butlin's for Christmas. One fellow remarked about a lad last year who had hot fat splashed on his arms while working – another lost his wage. One youth in a black cowboy hat, pierced ears with earrings, soon asked the driver to stop so he could 'nip round the back'.

Stopped at Toddington service station. Didn't have anything to eat or drink. 'Phoned John, but only put 2p in. Every time I tried to tell him the number to 'phone back the pips went.

One couple looked featureless – so nondescript. Others had identical bleached hair in curly styles. Arrived at Butlin's, Clacton, at 6 p.m. Reception door wide open, awful piped music playing 'White Christmas'. A gang of people from Glasgow arrived. One woman saying she was there in summer and sheets were damp.

We had to queue for form signing, and give a 20p deposit each for a chalet key. Taken to a building not fit for animals. Dingy, cold, no heating on. Hot water bottles on top of bunk beds minus corks. When filling them at a sink they became wet down the sides.

Door wouldn't lock and a lady and her daughter from Wakefield said they wouldn't sleep on damp sheets. Another said the corridor was littered with men at night. Supposed to be for 'ladies only'.

Joyce Park and daughter Judith teamed up with us to complain at reception. A hard-faced blonde (bleached) asked me who I thought I was talking to. I replied 'You!' and said that they weren't dealing with rabble when talking to me. Assistant personnel woman took us round to another lot of chalets. Up rickety wooden steps. Still dirty-looking bed linen, and cold. Then taken to self-catering residents'

Butlin's

HOLIDAY CENTRE
P.O. BOX 1
CLACTON-ON-SEA
ESSEX CO15 1AH
Telephone: CLACTON 24821

MRS H. & MISS H WHEELER   17·12·76
58 GREENHEAD LANE,
DALTON
HUDDERSFIELD, YORKS

Dear Sir/Madam,

We thank you for your acceptance of our Christmas offer of employment and confirm that everything is in order for your arrival.

I enclose your return Coach Ticket and would advise that the Coach will depart as follows:

Day and Date	WEDNESDAY 22nd DECEMBER 1976
Time	11.00.a.m.
Point of Departure	THE CALL.
	LEEDS.

We hope that you have a pleasant journey and we are sure that your period of Christmas employment with us will be a happy one.

PLEASE BRING YOUR COACH TICKET WITH YOU WHEN BOARDING THE COACH.

Yours faithfully,
for BUTLIN'S LIMITED,

Jarrett

DIRECTORS: Russell W. Evans, M.C. (Chairman), R.F. Butlin (Managing Director), O.E. Carter, F.H. Foulkes, A.L. Miller, F.C.A., T.H. North, N.E.E. Reper, R.L. Webb, A.T. Wright, President: Sir William E. Butlin, M.B.E.
Registered Office: 11 Hill Street, London W1X 8AE   Registered in England No. 323886

Left: Arrangements are finalised for spending Christmas at Butlin's.

Below: Receipts for coach travel to Butlin's, 17 December 1976.

BUTLIN'S HOLIDAY CAMP   195612

Received the sum of £2 00 ....shillings........ pence in respect of 'Miss H Wheeler - Coach fare Leeds
Date 17.12.76   Signed *Jarrett*

BUTLIN'S HOLIDAY CAMP   195613

Received the sum of £2 00 ....shillings........ pence in respect of Mrs H Wheeler - Coach fare Leeds
Date 17.12.76   Signed *Jarrett*

chalet. Icy cold in there too. Refused to stay. Took us in a Butlin's van to a guest house nearby. Said they'd give us a travel warrant the next day if we still felt the same way. A lovely, warm, clean place.

Couldn't unlock my case. Owner had to break the lock. With Joyce, Judith and Caroline for walk to the sea. Dark, but saw it vaguely. Pink eiderdowns. Not grubby mud colour.

THURSDAY 23 DECEMBER

Enjoyed breakfast at a round table surrounded by Christmas cards. A pleasant atmosphere. Nice person cooked the meal. Van collected luggage after we'd been back to Butlin's. The personnel manager, Mr Noble, had me in his office by myself. Told him I thought it morally wrong to have such conditions and became exceptionally angry. He replied that 'nothing would be right' for me and they had spent a huge amount on the dining room. I retorted it would have been better spent on basic necessities – such as corks for hot water bottles, and staff. And fewer tinsel and trimmings. He said I had to write to him with incidental expenses. He couldn't do anything but issue rail warrants for us.

Van driver drove so fast to Clacton station when I was turning round to get a modicum of pleasure from the fiasco by looking at the sea that I was hurled to the other side. All laughing. Telephoned John at the station and told him we were coming home. He rang the number back and said he'd 'phone Granville and let him know.

11.50 train to London. The porter said he'd heard lots of complaints about the camp this year.

1.30 p.m. Arrived at Liverpool Street station. Paid 75p each for taxi to King's Cross. Driver warned, 'Hold tight – it's my lunch time.' Train to Leeds left at 2.10 p.m. Packed. Had to haul cases through carriages – lost Joyce and Judith. A girl moved up so that Caroline and I could squeeze onto a seat next to her.

Talked all the way to Doncaster, where she left wishing us 'a Merry Christmas'. One chap fell full length in the aisle, one following nearly did, and his big boot heel caught a little black and white mongrel called Whisky – en route for Christmas hols – in its jaw. I asked its owner if the kick had displaced its teeth. She said no, it always had prominent lower teeth. Talked to it in comforting manner, but couldn't

'Let's hope the name on this shop won't be the verdict on Christmas dinner.'

help laughing. Changed at Leeds. Home 7.30 p.m. Granville had been invited to a party. Was wearing his fur hat and looked to be enjoying himself!

How glorious, what a relief, to join Prince the cat on the rug in front of the blazing fire – and forget our working holiday at Butlin's.

CHRISTMAS EVE

Breakfast with Granville and Caroline. John telephoned. Received the bat and ball for his cat. It had only had a walnut before (to play with). Granville shopping in town. Bought a 9 lb turkey, cost £6.99. John telephoned again before 2 p.m. Whispered he 'loves me dearly' – could I say so about him? Wished each other a Happy Christmas. Will I be at home over the holidays, in case he could 'phone?

Afternoon. Washing, cooking, prepared sherry trifle for tomorrow. Assistant from bead shop came with bread. Caroline had forgotten to collect it. Sarah brought Christmas card, Avon Blue Blazer talc for Granville, and box of notepaper and envelopes for me.

Evening. Granville, Robert and Elizabeth in car to Scapehouse pub. Caroline and I stayed in and watched a film on TV. When they came back, supper and watched carols from Burnley Church on TV.

Elizabeth and Robert have announced their engagement in tonight's *Examiner*. How misleading adverts can be – 'Work and play at a Holiday Camp this Christmas – and get paid for it.'

I'll pay a fortune teller before accepting glowing adverts another Christmas! In retrospect, entertaining elderly relatives is better. Those unsavoury characters boarding the coach in Leeds – Caroline and I could laugh about them while safely back home. A busload of convicts would have looked more reassuring to spend Christmas with. The elderly chap on the seat opposite confided he'd 'picked his coat up from a jumble sale a year ago for 10p'. It smelled more like a 100 years ago. His headscarfed 'missus' proudly told how her husband had 'done time – but working at Butlin's kept him out of mischief'.

And it was one way of making sure they had a Christmas dinner. 'It can be a bit nippy at nights in the chalets, but you won't feel it after a few jars,' she grinned knowingly.

Neither Caroline nor I were interested in 'jars'. Neither did we wish to be stand-offish, so how to react? And then those lads who swayed up the aisle desperate to relieve themselves before the coach had been on its way ten minutes.

'We've had too much Wallop,' they explained, sticking their tongues out at us when staggering back to their seats.

Over the years, what lucky escapes many have from a Christmas almost worse than death…

But then, reading about Christmases where nothing happens and everyone behaves impeccably is not very interesting to reread in diaries in future years.

CHRISTMAS DAY

Robert and Elizabeth in car to take mother to the Rose and Crown at Thurstonland. I cooked the dinner. Began with grapefruit cocktail and the wine that we brought back from the Grantley Hall weekend.

Afternoon. Presents round the Christmas tree in front room. Giving and receiving took all afternoon. We gave Elizabeth a white fluffy rug, a chunky yellow teapot, a coffee pot and a cream jug. Gloves for Robert. Caroline gave Granville and me her traditional stockings, each full of presents. Scarlet stockings edged with black lace. Mine included a scarlet tabard, and a *Writers' and Artists' Yearbook*.

Robert gave us a Cuckoo Clock. We had to re-hang it in hallway because it cuckooed every quarter of an hour and gave us a shock.

Also an old-fashioned pub-type mirror with advert for Pears soap on it. Hung that in living room. Imagine – we hadn't even one mirror when we married at first. Too busy looking at each other. After tea Robert and Elizabeth went for a walk while mother, Caroline and I read in comfy armchairs with a glorious log fire. Mother driven home by Robert at 10.45 p.m. Feel mean with her going back to a lonely flat. Pale blue sky and sunshine today. But cold.

BOXING DAY

Still a clear blue sky. Filled diary. Robert went for mother to go to Margaret's with us. We had the meal, beginning at 3.30 p.m. By 4.30 p.m. all in front room and Margaret said, 'Is there anything you want to watch on television?' She put *Tales of Beatrix Potter* on. John went to sleep. So did Robert. Mother couldn't hear, so conversation was more or less out.

She was obviously bored – said to Granville, 'Do you want to dance a jig?'

I retorted, 'Don't be silly.' Felt so utterly, frustratingly bored my head seemed to be going hot. John went out for a walk after E. and R. had done. I was glad to get away when we left at 7.45 p.m.

Robert kept putting his knife into his mouth when eating. Everyone so utterly alien to the type of person I enjoy being with. The only bit of the day I enjoyed was watching *University Challenge* at home, and being able to answer some of the questions. If I'm not flexing my brain I feel completely dead. Elizabeth and Robert went to a party at Mirfield later.

MONDAY 27 DECEMBER

After breakfast Granville did some washing, including curtains from Caroline's bedroom. Caroline and I then went for a walk to Castle Hill. Raining in the wind. Back via fields and Sharp Lane. Carried thick pieces of wood back. What a reception on reaching home! Granville had window open, which was steamed up. *Wide* open. He was ironing wet curtains, and the heavy bedspread, which has been on the line outside for days, was draped round the fire. Damp steam all over. Blew up in a rage left over from yesterday. Put the heavy red and white mass into big bowl in the kitchen. Then he was going to hang the sodden curtains in C.'s bedroom. I said we'd have been as well getting damp at Butlin's and being paid for it.

Cold turkey, pickles, Xmas cake and coffee at about 2.30 p.m. Then I re-ironed what G. had done.

Desperately, Granville tried a joke:

DINER: D'you serve crabs here?
WAITER: Sit down sir, we serve anybody.

Boom, boom.

Caroline and I filled in application forms for Grantley Hall courses, then she read. Granville seems unable to settle with a book. Thought about Trixie, next door's cat, which has been missing for seven weeks, when we heard dance music emerging from there. 'Its little grey heart would be bursting with unhappiness,' I said. When they got Sam and Sally, they were less bothered about it than ever. Mildred telephoned to ask us to go for New Year's Eve. 7 p.m. E. and R. came back from pantomime at Bradford. R. turned nasty when I said something about chaos *here*, let alone in the pantomime. He refused to say more.

Feel sick with fed-upness. 'Phoned Joyce Park (met at Butlin's). Read. Mother telephoned. Roll on writing days by myself!

WEDNESDAY 29 DECEMBER

Crisp, frosty. Walked to town, and back. Coffee and reading *She* and *Popular Gardening*. Also *Woman's Story*. All have letters of mine published inside. Relief to be by myself again. Joe Wood called for Authors' Circle workbook. When John telephoned he said 'every day became heavier and heavier over Christmas' – he missed me so much. Feels he could have been a writer if he'd been married to me. He'd have been so happy he'd have gone slightly mad! Talking to me has been like being reborn. 'Like the *Danse Macabre*?' I said. When the dead come dancing out of their graves.

I telephoned Jim Chadwick of the Dunkirk Association to ask if I can interview him about it. Invited me to a branch meeting.

THURSDAY 30 DECEMBER

Very cold. 1977 diary arrived for Caroline from John. 30p postage, first class mail (for future comparison of postal increases). To supermarket. Saw little gingery dog shivering tied to a post. Talked to it then asked a policeman if he thought the poor thing had been abandoned. We waited with it until its owner came. Walked back with her.

Afternoon. Re-typed page of Halloween article and letters. John 'phoned at 4 p.m. He pinched a copy of *She* magazine from his newsagent's counter to read my letter. Called him 'the Thief of Baghdad'. He's going to put it back on the stand tomorrow. Writing article about Christmas at Butlin's.

At home in Greenhead Lane, 1976.

NEW YEAR'S EVE

Lovely sunny day. Baked buns. Up fields to see mother. Took her an inch of shin beef, carrots and an onion to make herself a stew. Supermarket. Baked chocolate cake, made sherry trifle and a stew.

Evening. With Granville and Caroline on bus to Netherton. Mildred and Harold's. Talking, sherry and chocolates, then steak and kidney pie. Wine, coffee and after dinner mints. Granville had ordered a taxi for 1.30 a.m. The only one he could get was an Indian firm.

I had a conviction beforehand they wouldn't turn up. Wanting to be ready when taxi turned up, sat in boots and coats (and central heating) till 3 a.m. Didn't want to stay as Mildred suggested because Prince, the cat, would have been alone in house from 8 p.m. last night. Elizabeth sleeping at Robert's. Just as we were clambering into studio couch converted into a double bed (Granville on a camp bed base in a sleeping bag) at the side of us, a horn blasted outside. I told Mildred to say we'd gone. She flung open the window, snowflakes blew in, and he drove away.

I slept in my jumper and pants. Caroline in her underslip and Granville in shirt and underpants. What a motley crew – a glamorous finale to 1976. But at least we're all four still intact and alive, including Prince. Only physical drawback a stiff shoulder from carrying case last week and riding in a cold coach.

Goodbye 1976. I've liked you and disliked you – what now?

Difficult Guests

SATURDAY 23 DECEMBER

Foggy. Caroline to town first. Granville and I took both shopping trolleys. Collected turkey, about 8 lb, cost £6.02. Other shopping then as we were dragging them on Wakefield Road. Robert drew up in his car and drove us rest of the way back. He stayed for lunch. I opened a tin of soup from the hamper, and made open-bap sandwiches with tongue, lettuce, mango chutney, raw onions and mustard in wine (new kind). Coffee, Christmas cake and cheese.

Afternoon. Robert took G. to supermarket for more shopping, and Caroline to see Elizabeth. I did lots of washing up. Prepared liver and onions, potatoes in jackets, rice pudding. Brussels sprouts and broad beans. I baked ginger gem biscuits and sponge buns. Television: BBC is back from strike action but not Yorkshire television. Caroline out late with Janet.

CHRISTMAS EVE

Raining. Elizabeth, Robert and mother here for their presents and brought some for us. They left after coffee and mother had spoken to Annie on telephone about sharing a taxi. Read papers, made a stew. G. and I watched TV in evening. Granville's leg hurting and he has a cold starting. Prepared potatoes and Brussels sprouts for tomorrow.

CHRISTMAS DAY

Dull weather. Snow all gone with heavy rain. Looking for colander to put Christmas pudding in. Granville brought it out of the hut – where stray cats go. Had to clean it before use. Then we'd to look up how to cook turkey in 1902 cookery book. Annie's first words on arrival at 12.30 p.m.: 'Granville Wheeler, you haven't swept the leaves up from the path – I nearly fell.' So annoyed I stayed in kitchen and didn't go to greet her. Mother with her. Margaret and John here too. The former on a diet, and said John preferred a cooked meal at teatime. Then Annie said she didn't like the wine, and when I passed her to get the coal, remarked that I'd make a better door than a window.

I longed for the day to be over, as at one time I longed for it to go on forever. Audrey telephoned at 4 p.m. Bobby is terrified of the toy squeaking dog we sent, so she is going to take the squeaker out. Annie spoke to her. Rather tactless remark again, Philip having died in May, and Audrey's first Christmas as a widow: 'I am going to Crosland Moor tomorrow, but having another taxi as there will only be a skeleton bus service on.'

Desultory conversation of sorts till they went. Put nearly a full bottle of rum in mother's bag, turkey and sherry trifle for tomorrow. Worn out trying to please such difficult guests.

Muriel, Della and
Hazel, 1978.

BOXING DAY

Sunny. Pleasure at last listening to old Victorian songs on radio while getting ready
to go to Muriel Kelly's at Hepworth. G., Caroline and I walked to town, then bus
at 11 a.m. Walked from Jackson Bridge. Muriel and Della coming to meet us as
we neared cottage. She was thrilled with the 1979 *Writers' and Artists' Yearbook*,
which I gave her. Also a box of sherry-filled chocolates, and a biscuit bone for
Della.

They came for a walk with us before going back for coffee and biscuits. Then
Muriel chatted entertainingly and sang. Used to be in Huddersfield Choral, so
worth listening to. Much more enjoyable time than yesterday. Left at 4 p.m. to
walk for the 4.20 bus to town. We had sprouts, mashed potatoes, chicken and beef
for late lunch; trifle, tea and biscuits before. Walked home from town. Some rain.

Fried leftover potatoes and vegetables for tea, and finished the trifle. With a
great big log fire, all stayed in and watched TV. I filled diary in.

WEDNESDAY 27 DECEMBER

Awful dark, rainy day. Granville to work. Breakfast with Caroline. Wanda and
Trevor came. They all three went out for a drink to Lindley. Trevor kissed me and
wished me 'Happy Christmas'. Wanda and Caroline back here for lunch. Ironing
when John 'phoned at 1.30 p.m. After saying he'd had a quiet Christmas, said it
had seemed a long time since he spoke to me. Had it seemed so for me?

'I can't wear my heart on my sleeve forever,' he flared. Then: 'Sod you then!' He
rang off.

I, naturally, 'phoned Muriel. Jane Galvin from Authors' Circle called. Telling
her about the £15 letter in the *Sunday Mirror* – hers – under her married name.
She was thrilled, and 'phoned her dad. John 'phoned again at 4 p.m., with some
excuse about a police quiz to ask Caroline. Told him about Jane. He then said he'd
'catch up with my hectic life tomorrow'.

I almost weakened halfway through conversation to be like I used to be, but
didn't. Alan Brown then called with a box of chocolates for me. Eventually
managed to do more washing and prepare tea. Ironing sheets in evening. Felt
depressed. Especially as Caroline didn't go to the disco till 1.30 a.m.! The time
I used to be back home when young. Granville had to sleep in small bedroom.
Terrible snoring.

THURSDAY 28 DECEMBER

AGM Authors' Circle. Torrential rain. G. 'phoned to say John has won the £25
best sports letter. That's £35 altogether from the *Daily Star*. He wouldn't have
known the addresses but for me, but he's too mean to even send me the smallest,
cheapest Christmas present. How disillusioned I am about him. It's not the gift,
but the thought, to use a cliché. Tidying up most of day. Polished furniture, cleaned
mirrors and windows, changed bed round.

Almondbury Church, December 1978.

At 4 p.m. John 'phoned. Told him about my £10 from *Daily Star*, then about his win. He was so excited he shouted out to one of his colleagues to tell him. Then he asked if I was alone. Said 'I love you–'

I didn't respond. Then he asked if I'd be in in the morning, they're having a bit of a party in the office tomorrow afternoon. I asked, 'With plenty of mistletoe?'

He replied, 'Well, you're not bothered – hearts on sleeves and all that – touché.'

I said the prize would brighten his way home. He said *I* would.

Floods in Northern England.

Evening. To town. Halfway through the agenda at Authors' Circle in the library I made a few 'retiring' comments as president. Then Mildred Coldwell became president for 1979.

Prefer not to have the bother of conducting meetings.

SATURDAY 30 DECEMBER
Wendy and Caroline had breakfast late. (Wendy from London, here from Friday till New Year's Day.) They went to a disco again. Audrey telephoned just as they were leaving and I'd hoped to be able to relax and read papers and magazines. She talked till after 11 p.m. Cost no expense, Philip having died 'in harness' when a bank manager. She hates being alone. Wish Wendy didn't smoke. There's a stale pall of it in the mornings when I come down.

NEW YEAR'S EVE

Snow on ground. All morning baking, cooking beef, potatoes, cauliflower, and tidying up. Caroline and Wendy came down for lunch. All to Elizabeth and Robert's for tea. It isn't very warm there, especially when sliding doors are open. Record player was on with awful pop stuff. Had argument with Wendy – opera and ballads versus that din. Will be really glad when I'm on my own again, and these so-called 'festivities' have ended.

Caroline changed into pink satin tight trousers and black jumper and black boots, which she could hardly stand up in. They set off at about 9.45 p.m. to meet Janet and go to another disco. (Never know if I'll ever see her again.) Robert, Elizabeth, Granville and I had game of Scrabble then watched *The Good Old Days* from Leeds City Varieties.

Elizabeth had warned me not to be crying and emotional, but she had to go out of the room when someone sang 'Danny Boy'.

We left a few minutes after 1979 came in and I clung to Granville's arm as we slithered down the hill from their house. Wished a few people 'Happy New Year' as we walked on Wakefield Road.

Never imagined it would be like this, with no brother Philip.

Sickly Waves of Heat

CHRISTMAS EVE

White layer of frost up the fields. Caroline and I having breakfast when John 'phoned. She answered. Wished us Merry Christmas – will only be away two days. Perhaps he thinks I might expire if any longer. 'Phoned Mildred. Asked what time she is on Radio Leeds. Granville to bed before the Christmas Eve service was televised. Caroline and I in our dressing gowns till 1 a.m. Trying to pick pencils up with our bare toes. I said if we didn't manage to that awful man on TV last night would get us.

CHRISTMAS DAY

Perfect weather. Slight frost, bright sunshine, clear blue sky. Taxi arrived, driven by a handsome Pakistani, 12 noon. Mother was ready when we called for her, but Annie wasn't. I was enraged. Told her it would have been wrong had it been me. Tried to make excuse she'd had a visitor. I said she should have got rid of her. When we arrived at Margaret and John's, Granville, Caroline and I went for a short walk to regain my composure. I wore the velvet cloak Elizabeth gave me. Mother had difficulty eating. Fruit juice would have been easier than grapefruit for her. Granville was given thin socks the colour of dried mud. Headscarf for me, similar hue. Socks too short so Granville gave them to Caroline. She had given us the usual stockings full of presents after breakfast. Including slippers for G. and a pullover called 'Casual Affair'. Blue dressing gown for me, and a bowl she made at pottery classes. (On my desk to hold pens.) In the afternoon I read my story 'Old One Eye', which Annie had said she'd like to hear.

And she went to sleep before I'd barely started to read it. We watched *All Creatures Great and Small* and Mike Harwood's impersonations on colour TV.

Christmas card to Granville and
Hazel from 'Mama', 1979.

Buffet tea. Taxi came for us 8.50 p.m. £4.50 each way. Mother gave us £2 but
gave it back to her. Annie merely said she'd see Granville later. Stayed up watching
Parkinson on TV at home with a glorious log fire.

THURSDAY 27 DECEMBER

High winds and rain. Granville washing living room walls. I washed covers of
old books, cleaned photo frames. John 'phoned before 1.30 a.m. and Granville
answered. I'd just made herb tea, one of Caroline's Christmas presents to me.
After Granville had gone to town for some paint I began to feel quite ill. Sickly
waves of heat flowing over my head. Was peeling a banana when he came back.
We only had a scone with the herb tea as neither of us felt hungry. Granville said
the banana looked like my survival kit.

He made tea and chips. A small tin of chicken. I even felt too worn out to put
the kettle on. It has rained non-stop today and it's windy.

In bed I kept crying. The thought of a new decade is far from pleasant. Philip
will never have been in it. Elizabeth now far away. John will have retired from
work before it is over, and I bet I'll never hear from him again. Or if I do, rarely,
and certainly not every Monday to Friday at 4 p.m.

Granville, Robert Connolly
and Elizabeth, 1979.

Finally, before the 1980s are over I'll have reached my sixties! Oh, woe is me.
(Till something happens to snap me out of this mood.)

NEW YEAR'S EVE
Authors' Circle party here. Frosty, sunny. Busy all day preparing. Mildred,
Marjorie, Pauline Murray, Jack and Rena Sykes, Joyce Woodhouse, Muriel and
Della here. I'd intended having plenty of time to be with them, and supper about
11 p.m. – an hour before the New Year starts. But they announced they were
leaving at eleven. Dismayed and fed up that all the hard work and plans were
wasted. Jack gave us a bottle of sherry. Muriel and Della stayed the night. Della
slept in bed with her. We talked till about 3.15 a.m. So ended the 1970s.

Never thought Philip would never see the 1980s. But, as with dad, I will take
him with me into them, so he will never be forgotten.

Under a Sea of Work

FRIDAY 12 SEPTEMBER

To London Writers' Weekend, Granville didn't go. Walked from tube to Queen Mary College's halls of residence, South Woodford, with Mary. She'd had a lung shot away in the war, and had to keep stopping to get her breath. Dinner at 7 p.m. We sat opposite a lady in her sixties who had on her badge of writing interests 'Sex and Gardening'! Later that night she was bitten on her eye and looked a bit like a werewolf for the rest of the course.

P. D. James gave a talk on writing her crime books later. Talked to two ladies, both suffered from depression. One had 'lost' her vicar husband. The other, unmarried, had an unidentified lover, and is a great friend of Deanna Durbin, the film star and singer.

SATURDAY 13 SEPTEMBER

First talk by P. J. Barsby – 'Jack of All Trades, Master of None'. Pays to have his booklets printed, and publicises them by sticking papers about them on trees or anywhere. He was very impressed when I told him I'd had two articles in *The Sunday Times*. He said they all seemed to be by MPs and the like. Roy Lomax, who writes scripts for *The Two Ronnies* (and later asked to be my agent – but a recession on and nobody was buying). Louise Brindley seminar, then a cheese and wine party. With Alexandre Le Carpentier and his wife much of the evening.

SUNDAY 14 SEPTEMBER

Windy, bright day again. Ted Willis gave an excellent talk and John Gittens, of Robert Hale publishers, spoke on 'Names and Addresses'. Tom Watling drove Caroline, Eve Blezzard and a seventy-eight-year-old lady back to South Kensington.

Tea at Caroline's flat then she came with me to King's Cross. 5.50 train to Leeds. A man in the first class carriage came down the subway with me to make sure I found the right train – which was ready to go, so I went in second class as I hadn't time to look for the first.

Granville met me. Home in taxi.

[While Caroline and I were at the 1980 London Writers' Weekend, Granville had pencilled a weekend diary on bits of paper. Here it is.]

FRIDAY
6.10. Margaret.
  7.45. Bath. Knock at Door. A lad – went away. Rain and Gales.

SATURDAY
Rain – gales.
  12.30. Caroline rang.
  1.15. Up fields. Did washing and Ironing.
  5.00. Feel Lonley. [He never could spell!]
  10.20. Bed.

SUNDAY
Up 9 a.m.
  11.00. 'Phoned grandma. Had enjoyed fish.

[Poor old Granville.]

WEDNESDAY 10 DECEMBER
Cold, rainy. John now redundant. No more 4 p.m. telephone calls from the south to liven the days. A 'dead' feeling realising this is only the first of weeks forever without the daily laugh, row, or serious discussion with an intelligent male. All from him 'chuckling' – as he wrote in 1975 – after reading one of my letters in *Popular Gardening*. He telephoned and asked if he could send me some hollyhock seeds. Which progressed to an unseen telephone admirer – not *Monday Night at Eight*, the old radio programme, but a 'phone call every working day at 4 p.m. Back in 1975. Fact is certainly stranger than fiction. Only crude, beer-swilling Yorkshire dullheads to meet from now on. Rolled lots of old newspapers into firelighters.

Afternoon. Packed for overnight stay in Liverpool. Muriel 'phoned. Telling me about an article she has written called 'Loos I Have Known'. It gave me a much-needed laugh. Annie 'phoned asking which day she is coming here at Christmas – she thought Robert would be bringing her. Embarrassing – Elizabeth has said that they won't be 'chauffeuring everybody about'.

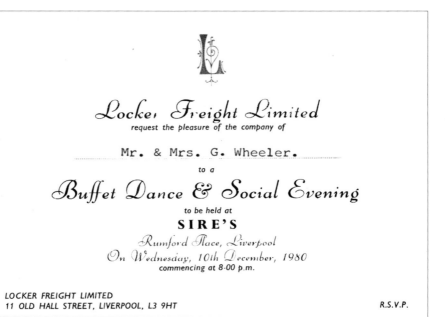

Locker Freight Limited
request the pleasure of the company of

Mr. & Mrs. G. Wheeler.

to a

Buffet Dance & Social Evening
to be held at
SIRE'S
Rumford Place, Liverpool
On Wednesday, 10th December, 1980
commencing at 8·00 p.m.

LOCKER FREIGHT LIMITED
11 OLD HALL STREET, LIVERPOOL, L3 9HT   R.S.V.P.

Invitation to 'Buffet Dance & Social Evening' at Sire's, 10 December 1980.

Granville came back from work to take me to town on bus. Not safe to even go down the lane in dark now, because of the Ripper.

In car to Central Hotel Liverpool, with Alan Brown. Buffet dance and Social Evening at 'Sire's' club. Went in taxi after changing into red velvet dress, black stockings and shoes. Didn't enjoy it. No one interesting to talk to. Even if there had been, couldn't have heard because of the deafening disco. Back to hotel in taxi after midnight.

Curfew shall ring tonight. In medieval days the curfew was rung at sunset from four London churches, after which 'no man shall be as daring as to go wandering about the City unless he be some man of good repute or his servant, and that with reasonable cause and with light'.

THURSDAY 11 DECEMBER
Enjoyed the hot cooked breakfast in the Liverpool hotel. Back to Huddersfield on bus. Shopping. Home. Took fish up fields for mother, then to supermarket.

Milder weather. Sunny when we left Liverpool.

Evening. Watched TV. Mrs Thatcher, Prime Minister, has been to Wales, where there were demonstrations about massive unemployment.

When will the hordes realise that it is they themselves – by demanding too high remuneration for shorter working hours – who have brought this state of affairs about?

But of course, self-help bodies are run by those affected, Alcoholics Anonymous by reformed drinkers and so on. But when the National Schizophrenia Fellowship advertised a post, one man wrote, 'I am in two minds about applying for the job.' [Joke quoted by Hazel Wheeler.]

TUESDAY 23 DECEMBER

Raining but mild. In car with Robert to supermarket then he went to a farm for a big bag of potatoes. To bank. A lady with a dog saying she's looking after two more dogs on Christmas Day – which would be better than last year with three undisciplined grandchildren. The potty in one corner – everything in a mess. After salad with Elizabeth and Robert I did more washing, including kitchen curtains. Which immediately blew off the line and fell in the mud.

Margaret 'phoned to thank me for presents. Hasn't anything for us – thought we'd decided not to exchange gifts last year. Trust me to forget! Made two lots of chips. Intended eating up salad left over from lunchtime. Waited and waited. Granville failed to turn up. Realised he wasn't coming, so ate two teas. Caroline arrived 7.45 p.m. Robert picked her up in town then returned to Meltham.

Buying slippers for Christmas? Did you know that the human foot resists standardisation, and more size grades are needed than in anything else a person uses? Shoes in Britain and the US are still ruled by a decree in 1324 when it was found the longest normal foot equalled thirty-nine barleycorns laid end to end. They called that 'size 13' and graded the rest down in one-barleycorn steps.

CHRISTMAS EVE

E. and R. left the boiled eggs I'd prepared – they only like scrambled. G. to work. They went to bring the turkey. £7.60 for a 10 lb one. Ages grating cabbage, carrots, nuts, raisins for a salad while Robert was in kitchen wrapping Elizabeth's presents. Sunny, windy.

Afternoon. Preparing for party. Elizabeth wanted people to wander in and out eating, not sit at the table. Granville forgot to bring the coffee back. Robert and Elizabeth to town to get some more shopping.

Car had to be taken to a garage this morning. Cost R. another £3. Ronnie Hill 'phoned to say he and Betty aren't coming. B. too tired after working all day in Sylvia's shop. Then when Laurie Stead arrived he was alone. His girlfriend has 'flu. Muriel and Della, who had been here for tea – we opened a tin of grouse and another of ham, and I'd made a big potato salad to go with it – had to leave just as Jim (Caroline's policeman friend) arrived from London. Joyce Woodhouse here.

> On the Twelfth Day of Christmas, the taxman sent to me;
> twelve bills for payment,
> eleven last reminders,
> ten cheques for signing,

'Even the tree was a skeleton.'

nine forms for filling,
eight large policemen,
seven VAT men,
six burly bailiffs,
five High Court writs,
four tax returns,
three more bills,
two summonses –
and a rebate of 21p.
    'The Businessman's Carol'

CHRISTMAS DAY
Snowing, hailing. E. and R. opening pillowcases full of presents. In bed while I cooked breakfasts. Robert went for mother and Annie. I asked if he'd like coffee when he returned (*not* instant). Said yes, then didn't come for it – he was playing about with new camera. Made me feel like a bloody skivvy. And I'd the lunch to see to as well. Joyce Woodhouse came. As she's vegetarian she didn't have turkey. Only onion soup then vegetables, cheeses, celery, biscuits. She left to go to her daughter's for tea. Gave us a round floral-patterned tray.

Cold turkey, coleslaw for tea, trifles, Christmas cake. Then Annie wanted to watch *Dallas* on TV so Caroline, Granville and I sat in front room reading. Bored stiff afterwards. Too late to do anything except wait for taxi to arrive at 9.30 p.m.

Annie gave G. and me £5 each – exactly the same amount she has given everybody else who do nothing for her. Crying.

I will honour Christmas in my heart, and try to keep it all the year.'
A Christmas Carol, Charles Dickens

BOXING DAY

Hail, snow. Thought we might be short of bread so had crisp biscuits with cheese, celery, grapes, pickles, coffee and fruit cake for lunch. Played record of Elizabeth singing nursery rhymes as a toddler. In car to Hepworth to see Muriel. She was outside getting coal in with Della. All went for a walk in a blizzard past a field full of black bulls. The nearest it felt to being Christmas was when Muriel sang before we left. Cooked tea when we returned, then another mammoth washing up. Caroline spent the evening reading her book, *The Woman in White*, which Jim had given her.

E. and R. went to a pub at Outlane. Said they'd spent money on one of those gambling things when they returned. They are very materialistic it would appear.

SATURDAY 27 DECEMBER *[extract]*

Robert washing his hair yet again. Gave Elizabeth another hot water bottle in bed. Couldn't move in living room so vacced upstairs. Wanda and Caroline called to see Caroline, also Janet.

All stayed for lunch. Made a festive buffet, with wine etc. When they went to the Stag to meet friends I washed up. More washing to hang out. Polished tables and tidied rooms. Utterly worn out. Don't even realise we've had Christmas. It's disappeared under a sea of work. Made tea when they came back. Robert pressed his trousers, not pulling the iron out till he'd finished. It was very hot for ages – they seem to waste things all the time.

Robert collected his mother and dad and sister to go out for a meal. Could hardly recognize her. She and Italian husband have separated. Then we were introduced to a rough boozy-looking chap, introduced as his uncle. What a lot Elizabeth has become involved with – makes me feel ill to think about it. And Robert tries to be so High and Mighty! Yet constantly lets himself down by his manner of behaviour. Had to have a glass of water in the Black Horse at Clifton – the others were on their second drink.

I didn't want another. Elizabeth asked, 'Are you alright?' Thought I'd better appear enthusiastic – after the meal, £50 for six, back to Bradley.

SUNDAY 28 DECEMBER

Cooked breakfast before E. and R. left. When hoisting washing over the creel Caroline, in the hallway, shouted, 'There's a card here from Elizabeth and Robert.'

I thought she'd said, 'There's a car here, Elizabeth and Robert...' Granville thought I'd hung myself in disbelief. Felt in a complete state of nervous and physical exhaustion. Robert can be very nasty. He told Elizabeth this morning – after all the presents she had bought him – that she had a spotty face. I told him no wonder she gets depressed. (He ought to look at his own rough lot.)

It will be three weeks on Tuesday since John spoke to me.

MONDAY 29 DECEMBER
Sunny, windy. Alone at last – with piles of sheets and other washing. Burst into tears when telling Mrs Shaw next door, also hanging washing out, about the awful time I've had. Richard up and down on his motorbike yesterday. The terrible noise. Loads of ironing. Muriel 'phoned.

That twirp next door revved into their garden path just when I'd gone to sleep. My heart was pounding wildly, head hot.

Detest situations I can't do anything about.

TUESDAY 30 DECEMBER
Supermarket. Dull. Windy.

Afternoon. Tired after last night. Downstairs reading papers then rolling them into firelighters. Granville asked them next door to ask Richard not to keep rising up and down. But he did. Even leaving the engine running while he disappeared inside the house. I flung the window open and yelled, 'Shut that bloody noise up!' Politeness gets you nowhere with some people.

Feel as though my nerves have all been exposed and are on the outside instead of inside. Kept nearly going to sleep after being woken up last night.

It was back to square one for the TV company after elaborately setting up a documentary showing a typical wedding. Ready to film, the bride's father asked, 'Will this be networked, or shown only in this area?' When told it would be seen nationwide, he said, 'Deal's off. My tax inspector in Manchester might see it and want to know where the money comes from to entertain 356 guests.'

NEW YEAR'S EVE
Gale force winds. On 9.27 train to Leeds with Granville. Bought eight coffee spoons, eight fish knives and forks, eight ordinary soup spoons. £18.24 altogether. First time in all our married life we've had special fish knives. Tried sitting on lots of armchairs but didn't decide on any. Either wood was too light or backs not high enough. Fish and chips for lunch in Whitelocks, oldest pub in Leeds. Even a waitress served us in a black dress and white apron, and was very friendly. Asked what we'd like for 'sweeties'. I had ice cream, Granville jam roll and custard. Looking at more carpets, suites and so on in Schofields, then coffee there. Home on train. Crab soup, salad, fresh fruit salad for late tea. Watched film about the

Queen Mother's life again, then *City Varieties Show* from Leeds, including Danny La Rue.

Crying. Muriel telephoned as Big Ben was pealing in the New Year to wish us a Happy New Year. Talking with Granville in bed before going into my own. (Snores arrangement.) Upset because nobody is romantic with me anymore.

Wonder what will happen in the future about John? If our relationship – if only a telephone one – is over forever, now he is not working. Can what I dreaded all these years have really happened – and so prematurely, too?

Men in bowler halts. Briefcases. New Year Honours list. 'I'm beginning to think I've been passed over – several of the knighthoods were in the class below me at school.'

Try Something Different this Christmas

The best part of keeping diaries is reading when the year is over and reliving 'past times'. On Friday 13 November I went to a writers' weekend in Scarborough. Ken Foster discussed non-fiction. Another man said he wrote for a beekeeping journal – how should he get then to pay anything? I suggested he wrote to them to say he was fed up of being stung! Playwright Alan Ayckbourn was the guest speaker.

Ken Forster talked about trade contests. Had recently won a Mini Metro, while Geoff won £1,000 some years ago with an Ajax competition. His slogan: 'Ajax goes round in ever *degreasing* circles.'

Geoff Pike from Melton Mowbray suggested I go outside with him for a walk at midnight. I didn't. He wasn't born till 1948!

Even though competitions may not be as numerous as in 1981 all firms are willing to consider superb slogans. Try writing some for a party game this Christmas – could get you out of the Credit Crunch.

Over the years I won many – and using your brain keeps the cobwebs and senile dementia at bay, besides boredom and being driven crackers at Christmas by the same boring old stories. Try something different this Christmas – for your brain and sanity.

For instance, 'A crossword shared is better than a cross word shared.'

Made that up now, for *Crackers at Christmas*.

Hazel with Alan Ayckbourn at the Scarborough Writers' Weekend, November 1981.

A Bit Out of It

WEDNESDAY 23 DECEMBER

Waiting for John Bell to call in his car to collect mother. Deep snow in garden. At Leeds station a big Christmas tree was lit and a band was playing carols. Granville and I had the big new navy shopping trolley, which I pushed with my clothes in. Granville had his case and mother's. We propelled mother, highly rouged and in fur coat given by Audrey, to the train. The coat had weathered umpteen Christmases by the look of it. A bit furless. Obviously past its best. But it had huge lapels, and in the crush of people I was worried how mother would manage the high train step without slipping down the gap.

Safest way was for me to get on the train first, then grab her shoulders perhaps. Leaning forward I hoisted the big fur lapels up – and mother's face disappeared completely in the coat at the crucial moment. A muffled, agitated voice cried, 'I can't see anything now!'

Like the song a bit – 'With her head tucked underneath her arm/At the midnight hour.' But mother's was obliterated by the coat. Hysterical with laughing I nearly let go. Then Granville came to the rescue and helped the thin, fur-coated body onto the train.

A psychology student from Hong Kong already seated was helpless with laughter as well. So was mother when once she saw the light of day again. The young man from Leeds University was going home to Hong Kong for Christmas. Mother sat by him, and the sight and remembrance of the drama with the headless figure in a mangy fur coat kept us all laughing hysterically throughout the journey. A porter had been there with a wheelchair in case mother needed it – but instead of pushing mother in it, Granville nearly sent me flying as he hurled past with our cases on the wheelchair.

Hilda in Broadstairs, Christmas 1981.

Caroline was supposed to meet us at the station, but no sign of her. A call was put out over the public address system. She had been waiting somewhere else. But she turned up in the nick of time for the train to Broadstairs. Caroline had made sandwiches, which we shared with a railway man who was sitting by me. Caroline accompanied mother to the lavatory on the train.

Mother never sits on public toilets in case she 'gets something'. So what with that and the swaying of the train in motion, the hem of her new green dress was wet on her return. I'd thought it too good to be true to get so far without mishap.

Arrived at Broadstairs station about 5 p.m. Granville went to 'phone Elizabeth, who came for us in her car. Casserole for our first meal there. I slept in bunk bed, Granville in another.

Mother in the bedroom, which will be the baby's when born in May.

CHRISTMAS EVE
Raining. Pouring like a torrent down the gutter as mother emerged, struggling, from the car. An event for her to ride in one. In a café for coffee. Looking for slippers for mother. £4. I bought red earrings, 35p. Sandwiches at Elizabeth's, then Robert, Granville and I took Caroline in his car to St Margaret's Bay Holiday Camp, where she will work as a waitress during Christmas. Another girl was to share the chalet. Robert and I went with them in driving snow to see it. No sooner

were we in than the girl got an electric shock – she switched the wall heater on with wet hands. I pleaded with Caroline not to stay, even offering to give her the money she hoped to earn rather than have her killed. But she stayed.

When we arrived back at The Maples, Elizabeth and mother looked in sulky moods. Elizabeth told Granville mother had 'driven her crackers' repeating the same remarks. *She* only has it once or twice a year. After tea we watched TV. Theirs is a colour set. Mother kept dropping to sleep.

CHRISTMAS DAY

In car to St Peter's Church. Mother had safety pins on the backs of her green gloves! Her motto has always been 'Be Ye Prepared'. And some inside her coat. A very pleasant vicar, smiling much of the time. He invited anyone who may be spending the day alone to join him for tea at 3.30 p.m. in the vicarage. Shaking hands with him on the way out, I remarked how I'd like to be alone so I could go to the vicarage! In car to the Frigate pub by the harbour. Mother had two rums and pep, and we talked with some 'cockneys' who were staying at the Bickenhall Hotel, Edgar Road, Cliftonville, for Christmas. Spoke to a dog in the pub. Owner says it prefers whisky to beer.

Back to house. Christmas cake, cheese and coffee, then exchanging presents. We gave E. and R. a green circular tablecloth with red berry pattern on white edging, a Christmas printed tea towel, an Estée Lauder make-up set, Vidal Sassoon shampoo and comb for Robert, a Wedgewood rabbit-patterned plate and a sponge for the baby-to-be. Granville gave £30 towards food, and a bedside book.

They gave me a book, *Christmas Fare*, and pyjamas for Granville. Mother a 'Friendship Book' and I gave her a plastic pinafore with a big golliwog on the front. And Lentheric perfume. (Which I hope will obliterate the TCP.)

Dinner – turkey, vegetables, wine, fresh fruit salad. Then watched TV. I read *Curious Facts*, a book Caroline had given to Robert. Elizabeth had heartburn and indigestion.

BOXING DAY

In car. Drinks at a pub in Cliftonville. A drive then sandwiches at The Maples. After the evening meal we watched the first half of *Gone with the Wind* on TV.

SUNDAY 27 DECEMBER

Snowing in the rain. Granville and I walked to the Frigate again, leaving the others reading the papers. We talked to two couples from Hertfordshire who were staying in a hotel where the electricity had been off all Christmas Eve, and related lots of other bizarre happenings. After lunch at E. and R.'s, Elizabeth, mother and I drove to St Margaret's Bay to collect Caroline.

Elizabeth wouldn't ask directions. As a result we missed the correct turning and ended up going down a series of dark and dangerous bends on the road.

Elizabeth and Robert
waiting for their first baby.
Christmas 1981.

Then the car stalled – curses – eventually found the holiday camp. I went inside
the ballroom to find Caroline. By which time she had gone to reception. Relieved
when we arrived back at 43 The Maples safely! All watched the second half of
Gone with the Wind on TV.

MONDAY 28 DECEMBER
Dull weather. Robert, Elizabeth, Granville and mother in car to Canterbury.
Mother was in a panic on an escalator, so a man at the bottom held his hands
out to help her and she embraced him fervently. No need for mistletoe! Caroline
and I didn't go, as not enough room in car. We washed our hair, coffee, walked to
Frigate. I bought two ploughman's lunches. Guinness with mine, orange juice for
Caroline.

We enjoyed it. Walked back by the sea. Elizabeth drove Caroline to the station. I
went with them – Caroline for the 3.18 back to London.

After the evening meal Robert drove us all to The Moonlighters pub at Peglar's
Bay. A waste of time and money because there was no one to talk to, certainly no

'Typical Granville scenario.'
December 1981.

one approaching mother's age. So I felt acutely conscious that she must feel 'a bit out of it'.

Tried to interest Robert in writing plays and children's stories.

TUESDAY 29 DECEMBER

Foggy. Robert driving, Gillingham then Maidstone. Granville promised to buy them a pram. Had to wait in rain until place available for parking the car. Fish and chips in Littlewoods. Stupid place. Not even anywhere to clean my teeth.

Left mother resting on a chair in Boots chemists while we others were looking at prams. Then we forgot where we'd left her. Eventually Elizabeth and Robert decided on a mushroom-shade corduroy pram with a rounded hood. £113.52. That was *without* a safety mattress or shopping tray underneath. Very different to the drab, second-hand grey pram that I was given by Grandma Wheeler in 1954. Elizabeth had prepared a casserole and it was ready in the self-timing oven on our return.

WEDNESDAY 30 DECEMBER

Mild, blue sky. First sunshine of the holiday. Robert drove us into Broadstairs harbour, parked the car while we walked along the promenade. To let mother see the sea. Her stocking was wrinkled, so she sat on a seat and tried to hoist it up with a safety pin. Elizabeth and Robert came onto station platform to see us off.

10.18 to Victoria station. Mother was getting in the taxi backwards and we only just managed to stop her sitting on the floor, legs flailing wildly. To King's Cross. A lorry driver looking out of a window behind was laughing – so were we. Caroline met us there for a final few minutes. I'd been 'relieved' that mother didn't want to use the lavatory on the train – but it cost 5p at King's Cross (I used to think an 'old' penny exorbitant). Not as pleasant a journey. Snow on the fields again as we sped northwards, knowing mother would be alone again shortly. She was sulking a bit when we tried to get her to say what she would do about her pension and Mrs Ellison.

At Wakefield station the driver got out to go to the front of the train. When it set off again I kidded mother that he'd given it a push and no one was driving. She believed me.

Water flooding down steps at Huddersfield station when we arrived. Probably melting snow. Taxi home to Greenhead Lane, £1.65. Abdul, the Pakistani driver, helped mother into the house up the slippery, snow-covered garden path. She kept falling asleep as we watched TV by the gorgeous log fire. Chips and fried onions for a quick tea. Mother slept in small front bedroom.

Grandparents-to-be Hazel and Granville in Broadstairs, Christmas 1981.

NEW YEAR'S EVE

Thick snow still all over, except middle of roads. Mother got up at 6.30 a.m. then returned to bed after putting her false teeth in. We all had breakfast at 7.45 a.m. I was worn out – every time I spoke she said 'Pardon?' Then said it must be the snow making her deaf. Granville got some food for her to take back to the flat.

I did loads of washing. Mother had forgotten to pack her shoes and was left clinging onto the back of Granville's coat down the slippery path. I was hysterical with laughing – then came in and burst into tears at what condition my once bright and vivacious mother was in. She slept in her stockings even though I'd put four hot water bottles in the bed.

Afternoon. Walked to town with Granville. Sometimes on piled-up snow on pavement, or in roadway. Took new shopping trolley back to shop because some stitching is loose. Owner wasn't there, so they refused to refund. Bought red 'K' shoes. £14.99. Walked home.

After tea Edward Adkins telephoned to ask if we would like to go to his house for the evening. I stopped ironing, had a bath, and dressed in black and white tartan kilt, red jumper and black cardigan. New white fur half-length coat. Foggy and icy outside. Pauline Murray was there also. We talked, had drinks, watched Hinge and Bracket on TV. Singing. Sausage rolls, sandwiches, mince pies, Christmas cake and coffee. Tia Maria to drink as Edward and Granville kissed Pauline and me at midnight, as 1982 ousted sad 1981 away forever.

Left Netherton at 12.30 a.m. in Edward's car. Foggy. We told him not to bother driving up the lane. Walked that bit. My main wish – one of them – for 1982 is to talk on the telephone again with John.

Feel as though all my one-time friends and acquaintances have disappeared this year. Have not enjoyed 1981 much, and can't see any year being right unless something happens so I can talk with John again.

NEW YEAR'S DAY

Frost, fog, icy roads. Ironing and listening to radio. Talk by Alistair Cook recounting some events and sounds of 1981.

1985

The Scarlet Woman

THURSDAY 19 DECEMBER

At Broadstairs, Elizabeth and Robert's. When Abigail was getting ready to dress as a fairy for the playschool party I asked where the jumpers were that I'd knitted for her. 'Daddy threw them in the dustbin,' she replied. She said Elizabeth had too, because they weren't pink and they didn't like them.

I felt awful. Was going to pack the skirts I've knitted and come away as soon as Elizabeth and Robert returned from Brighton.

SUNDAY 22 DECEMBER

On my pillow slip is printed, 'A kiss on the nose does much to turn aside anger.' I told Robert yesterday that I was glad Granville had had thrombosis as it had stopped him from drinking too much. Said 'Goodbye.' Had gone a few miles when Granville realised he had forgotten his anorak. Had to go back for it.

A long way on South Circular Road in heavy rain. To Caroline's at Chiswick. I rolled car window down to ask a taxi driver the way. He thought I had said 'Merry Christmas' and replied, 'The same to you.'

Granville had to get out and dodge traffic to go across to a pub to use the lavatory. Lovely and relaxing to be at Caroline's. Alan arrived for tea.

CHRISTMAS EVE

On tube to Richmond. Shopping, back to Caroline's flat. She drove us to Alan's maisonette at Denham. Meal there. Alan had put presents in crackers for us. Big Christmas tree with everyone's presents round the base. Alan and Caroline diving their hands into a big cardboard box full of his grandma's old Christmas trimmings. Then fixing them round the walls. There's a lovely big deep settee that

Above left: Abigail ready for the playgroup's fancy dress party, Christmas 1985.

Above right: Granville, Hazel and Caroline spend Christmas 1985 at Alan's in Denham.

I commandeered as soon as I saw it. The hyacinth bulbs we gave Alan are on the table at the side of the fire. There's an open staircase, which I was a bit wary of at first. There's a huge thick rope to pull instead of the modern thing on the lavatory side. Alan likes old-fashioned things – so do I. But glad he hasn't a cess pit.

At 11.30 p.m. he drove us to the village church service. When coming out, the vicar shook hands and remarked, 'It's nice to have the odd scarlet woman here for a change!' I had my red coat on and black velvet Laura Ashley beret.

Coffee and Christmas cake at Alan's before sleeping in double bed.

CHRISTMAS DAY

Raining. All the presents round the Christmas tree. Every time Caroline gave him one Alan kissed her. Caroline gave Granville and me a red, black-lace-edged stocking each full of presents. Coffee and mince pies, records. Caroline and Alan cooking turkey, vegetables, followed by Christmas pudding. An enjoyable change – after all these years – not to be in the kitchen myself.

About 5 p.m. Alan and Caroline went to his parents' home some miles away. I made a salad for Granville and me. Only a small black and white TV set there, so felt a bit 'flat' on our own. Would have liked to meet Alan's family. Caroline thinks there were probably too many people there for us to be invited.

BOXING DAY
Pouring with rain all day. Alan brought some 1925 copies of *Punch* magazine and old newspapers for me to look at. Caroline and Alan made the meals.

FRIDAY 27 DECEMBER
Sunny. Caroline drove us to Oxford Street before going to work. Bought her a yellow handbag (£4) and a red one for me. To Laura Ashley sale. Too crowded to try dresses on, so just bought a brown and black striped one reduced to £12, a turquoise one for Elizabeth (£25), and many others. Caroline made a Beanfeast shepherd's pie for us all when Alan returned from work.

SATURDAY 28 DECEMBER
Granville, Alan, Caroline and me in her red car ('Furry') to Brent Cross. I gave them £10 each, and paid for our lunches. All from Annie's legacy to me.

Felt lovely to be able to give something to them. Alan bought a white Christian Dior scarf with his. Back to flat mid-afternoon. Takes years to pay off moneylenders – hope we are never in such a terrible situation again. I had a bath then changed into new black £28 Laura Ashley dress, red stockings and new red shoes, £49. Never paid as much before, but as I never pay for hairdressers or anything I don't see why I shouldn't for once. To friends for the evening.

SUNDAY 29 DECEMBER
Very cold but perfect otherwise. Lovely blue sky, sunshine. Caroline dressed in trousers, jumper, and white boots. Flying to Barbados from Heathrow. Alan driving her there. Granville and I in Beauty up the M1.

Home about 2 p.m. Among Christmas cards one from Jack Sykes, saying the Authors' Circle is 'dull as ditchwater' without me – no arguments, no fun, and few in print. Caroline's flight delayed because of frost – she 'phoned as we came in from the car.

No water in taps – frozen up and house like an iceberg. Lit fires in both rooms and unpacked. Baked potatoes in jackets and baked beans for tea after Granville brought pans of water in from Armitages next door. 'Phoned Alan to thank him. He's feeling lonely without Caroline. 'Phoned Elizabeth. Read *The Sunday Times* and watched TV.

MONDAY 30 DECEMBER
Still no water. Pipes frozen up. Granville to work then home 10 a.m. armed with two electric fan heaters. One put in kitchen, one down cellar steps. Not a scrap of use. I heated some of water from bucket in bathroom and kept throwing it at pipe by drain in back garden.

After sandwiches for lunch took two big pans and knocked at neighbours' houses. All three out, or didn't answer. Kept bringing coal up from cellar to keep fire in front room going as well as living room.

Granville and the local boys in
Greenhead Lane, 22 January 1984.

Brought panel of water in with Richard Armitage. Used some for the birds and
to wash my hair. 'Phoned Muriel.

NEW YEAR'S EVE
Walked to town. Bought blue cotton trousers in Marks and Spencer, £14.99, and
blue velvet dress for Abigail reduced to £3.99. Bought food, then walking home
by Ravensknowle Park when Granville and Beauty cruised up. G. had come home
because he'd 'phoned and wondered where I was.

He opened the front door then came back to lift shopping trolley out. As I walked
up the hallway, appalled to see a mouse scurrying by refrigerator. Obviously ran
in when door was left open. G. went to Margaret's at Golcar to bring bulbs and
bowls back. He came home because I was frightened of being in with the mouse.
After not seeing it again I gained courage and baked in the kitchen.

Evening. Granville saw it again. Alan Bird telephoned. He's spoken to Caroline.
She says it's very hot in Barbados.

What a way for 1985 to retreat – scared stiff to go into the kitchen in case a
mouse appears.

Ghostly White Fingers

CHRISTMAS EVE

Up at 4.40 a.m. Packed cases into Beauty. Left about 6.30 a.m. for the drive to Denham. Alan was cleaning the bath. Caroline had been shopping. Milder than at home. Granville and I went for a walk. After lunch Granville slept on couch. Then we all went to see if there were any scarlet berries. Very muddy but enjoyable. Went to church about 11.30 p.m. John Mills, the actor, and his wife were there. Presents are round the Christmas tree as last year.

CHRISTMAS DAY

Sunny. We exchanged presents from stockings and red pillow slips we'd taken to put Alan's and Caroline's in.

A perfectly cooked turkey lunch, then in car to Alan's parents' home for evening meal. His grandma there as well. Such a change for us to be the guests, and not the harassed hosts.

They put a video on, a sailing holiday they had. Not my favourite pastime watching yachts and boats slowly manoeuvring along – but a pleasant evening nevertheless.

Frosty when we left, and car window iced over. Caroline had to wear her old short fur coat with the fur rubbed off the right shoulder because of seat belt, since her new fur coat had been stolen.

BOXING DAY

Alan drove us to Southwater near Horsham, to old friend Margaret Napier's. She and her daughter Hazel (named after me) had just had a row about Hazel's married soldier boyfriend when we arrived. Margaret had cracked Hazel across her face!

Halifax Authors'
Circle's 1986 Christmas
party. Hazel sits with
Irish writer Bernard
O'Sullivan. Granville
plays with Hilda
Gledhill's earrings.
Cynthia Hand is on the
far right.

We had a buffet lunch then Granville, Hazel, Jan the dog and I went for a walk. Saw the vicar. Asked him to call and talk to Margaret. In the afternoon Hazel pushed the chair with Margaret in it, and it went skimming across the room. Caroline couldn't stop laughing for ages.

Turtle the cat had a red ribbon around its neck. So did Jan, who amused everyone by pawing furiously at an upside-down plate, trying to right it again. Then Jan did her 'blanket dance' again. Left about 4.30 p.m. A meal at Alan's in the evening.

SATURDAY 27 DECEMBER

Alan to work. Caroline drove us to Brent Cross Shopping Centre for 9 a.m. Frosty at first. Laura Ashley sale. Caroline trying most on as I'd promised to buy her a coat to make up for the one she's had stolen. Bought her a red corduroy dress, a navy and white check suit, a velvet collar and buttons, a green-flowered long dress. That cost £22. Over £100 altogether. Also a black reefer jacket (£30) – but enjoyed being able to buy them for her for once without undue worry about prices.

Caroline, 1986.

MONDAY 29 DECEMBER
Fine, mild. In Beauty to Leeds. Laura Ashley sale first. Party dress for Abigail – £18. Some had been £55, exactly the same. Schofields, Pringle pullovers for Granville at £16.50 each. I'm paying for everything. Salad and coffees there. Sat by an eighty-three-year-old Viennese lady. She'd had 'visitors' for Christmas – Mozart, Haydn, Beethoven, all classical music. By herself, but a lovely time with the music. Duvet cover and pillow slips for double bed reduced to £25. Bath mat £4.50. Two bath towels £8.50 each.

Home. Raining about 3 p.m. Christmas cake, cheese and coffee. Audrey 'phoned. In Beauty to sale preview at Peter's in Huddersfield. Bought red dressing gown reduced to £20, turquoise one £18. And two sets of vests and pants.

Harold Macmillan, one-time Prime Minister, died tonight aged ninety-two.

TUESDAY 30 DECEMBER
Showery, blustery, mildish. Shopping in town. Ordered curtains at Allan's. Home for lunch. Granville did some washing. Walked to Waterloo for Dr Selbie to see my sore 'ring' finger, which I hurt before Christmas putting hand into shopping trolley. A metal piece had rammed into it. Doctor Selbie prescribed antibiotics and said keep it out of water as much as possible (reason G. did the washing). What do people do who live alone? Then Granville had to lie on table – or examination bed – with his trousers off. He told me not to look, but Dr Selbie said, 'Come and look here Hazel!' I was confronted with a couple of small red cracks in Granville's most intimate rear part! Pruritus. He had to get cream to anoint it.

Putting cases away Granville dropped a light bulb and it broke into small pieces over bedroom floor. Had to vac again to make sure none left to get into my feet. Winnie telephoned. Knitted some of royal blue mohair jumper.

NEW YEAR'S EVE
Fancy dress party at Spiritualist Church (white sheet?!). Sunny, blue sky, windy. In fact, a glorious morning. Baked a lemon cake while Granville went to collect curtains. Poppy-patterned, reduced to £17.90. Two cushions 99p each. Cocoa at home then to Wakefield in Beauty. Laura Ashley sale. But disappointed it was not clothes, only paints and wallpaper. Bought remnants and stationery set, £2.50. Looked round other shops. Bought four Victorian prints, £18 altogether. Home for salad, coffee and lemon cake at 2 p.m. Walked to Lodge's supermarket at Waterloo. Still bright weather.

Draught coming into living room from cellar. Granville dared to say, 'If only I'd let him put that stuff round the door.' I exploded with anger. Thin useless stuff like ghostly white fingers, which he drapes over every crevice as winter approaches (given the chance).

The times I've seen them waving from bedroom windows coming up Greenhead Lane... Why the Hell aren't doors made to fit to start with? Only makes them difficult to open, and tempers inflamed. Put red dressing gown over clothes to keep out the draught. Granville instead fixed old mustard-coloured velvet curtain outside living room door.

He was outside when I floundered through curtain, forgetting I had red fluffy dressing gown on. He exploded with laughter – said I looked like Father Christmas coming out of Santa's Grotto. Decided against Spiritualist Church party. Watched an excellent short story (adaptation on TV) by Thomas Hardy, *The Day after the Fair*.

At midnight told Granville the year had arrived when I would disintegrate (sixty next April!). He replied he's cracking up already (small cracks in his rear end).

As long as he can keep on cracking out laughing we'll survive.

Like a Match to a Tinderbox

FRIDAY 18 DECEMBER

Mild. Hung washing out – then it rained. Upset when postman handed over a parcel from Audrey. Brut talc for Granville, and aftershave lotion. He doesn't like the smell of Brut. A huge black and white scarf for me. Too large to wear as a scarf, and shawls are outdated. Crying. Tried new boots on. The left one hurts by my ankle, as it did when I wore it at the party (they are knee-length). [Later, I liked the scarf and wore it at Christmas.]

SATURDAY 19 DECEMBER

Fine, mild. Took boots back to Peter Lord shop. Given the £49.99 back. Bought a lot of yellow squeaking balls at 49p each for dogs, colouring books for Abigail, Adele and Charlotte.

Home for lunch. Granville took box of three soaps (£2.99), a ball, a tin of cat food and a diary for Rita Holroyd. Three carraway buns and piece of Christmas cake (home-baked) for old Mary Taylor. She wasn't there – had a fall not long after her birthday. Now in hospital.

Packing for going to stay at Caroline's new flat tomorrow.

SUNDAY 20 DECEMBER

Driving to Uxbridge. Alan and Caroline had gone to Ashford to collect Abigail. All three of them were there when we arrived, flustered, after Granville had taken a wrong turning.

Boiling hot with central heating on. Alan hardly spoke, sat with eyes closed – how very boring. After tea there they went to his cottage at Cookham.

We put the small borrowed TV set on a small chair so it would be off the floor. That left only the small wooden armchair to sit on apart from the settee. Watched TV and read *The Sunday Times*.

MONDAY 21 DECEMBER
Caroline and Abigail here by 9 a.m. To park car at Turnham Green. Nothing to interest Abigail there, apart from a shop showing antique toys. Another tube to Embankment. Collected tickets for *The Wind in the Willows* at the Vaudeville, then to Hamleys toy shop.

Bought a rabbit bride and bridesmaid in a box. £8.99 for Abigail. Part of the Maple Town Collection.

To Country Life, a vegetarian establishment near Regent Street. £2.99 for a main meal, from lots of choices. Abigail only wanted a baked potato and bits of raw carrot. I'd have preferred a Gilbert and Sullivan concert or a musical to *The Wind in the Willows*.

Abigail stayed at the flat after. She didn't like sleeping in the small bedroom at Alan's with all those pots of paint, saws, and other clutter. Nowhere to get undressed or dressed and no mirror. She wouldn't watch the carol service and was in a bit of an awkward mood.

TUESDAY 22 DECEMBER
Caroline arrived. Parked car at Chiswick again. Tube to South Kensington. Harrods toy department with Abigail after buying red boots for her, £22.50. Also £2.95 for another little bear in a pinafore. 'Am I allowed to have anything?' she'd asked (after buying all that yesterday).

Who could resist? Salad lunch in Harrods. Then Abigail tried a Father Christmas sleeping suit on, complete with hat and white pom-pon. Cost (reduced) £15.75. She had been entranced by a robot with an alluring voice. She ran across in her suit, and stood before it.

'Who have we here? Little Miss Christmas?' he said. Abigail kissed the robot.

In the changing room, she excitedly said, 'I hope the robot doesn't come in here!' Then: 'Actually – I hope he does.'

Tea at Caroline's flat, then she went to Alan's. Abigail and I talking for ages at bedtime. I had to remove plants from the window ledge. She thought they looked weird. Then she couldn't bear to look at me – I looked like a ghost in the dark.

Granville snoring loudly.

WEDNESDAY 23 DECEMBER
Alternate fog and sunshine. In Beauty, taking frequent wrong turnings, to take Abigail back to Ashford. She wore her new red sheepskin boots and pink fluffy coat. Telling her about our 'family tree', mother, Boroughbridge, *The Milliner's Apprentice* – my book about her life there.

No sooner back, bouncing on the bed with Charlotte and Adele, than her nose was bumped. Tears. Then she pulled the twins away from Granville, accusing him of having dirty hands. Elizabeth smacked her. Abigail retired upstairs. As we went after her she slammed the bedroom door on us. Could have seriously damaged our

SIZE 2,3Y   M4 401 246402   PRICE £23.75

£15.75

Harrods

TRIMFIT   3678   RED   L4

Abigail (five), Christmas 1987. *Inset:* The sales tag from Harrods.

fingers. First time in my life I tapped her 'behind' – being so nasty when we spent so much on her, and did all in our power to give her a happy time. When Elizabeth and Caroline were young they *never* behaved badly with their grandparents. Not *my* side of the family coming out in such behaviour! She refused to have any lunch. Mackerel, salad, coffee and crunch.

Elizabeth and Abigail went into the town to collect Robert's mother. Granville took Adele and Charlotte for a walk. I cleaned kitchen sink and washed worktops. Left about 4.20 p.m. to return to Caroline's Uxbridge flat.

Alan is a bookshop manager, yet when *University Challenge* was on, he didn't know what 'falsehood' meant. Thought it must be some kind of hood people wore in the war. Nicknamed him 'Falsehood' after that.

CHRISTMAS EVE

Mild, fine. Parked Beauty then G. and I walked into Uxbridge to get more shopping. A flask for Molly (Robert's mother) £2.99, green towel for Elizabeth, small one for Ann and Andrew – Robert's brother and wife – and dried apricots and other items such as vegetarian mincemeat to take to Ashford on Boxing Day. Three soaps with pictures of Care Bears on, and three coloured sponges. Lunch by ourselves in Caroline's flat, then packed to go to Alan's.

Busy on the M4 to Cookham, and some mist. White rice (Granville hates it – more used to rice puddings in his Colne Valley childhood) and stir fry vegetables for tea. Followed by blackberry crumble.

I read an extract from my 1952 diary for Alan's entertainment. Read magazines. Walked to church for a Christmas Eve service which began at 11 p.m. Alan walks on the inside when with Caroline – he ought to know that is wrong. The gentleman should be on the outside to protect the lady. Walked back afterwards.

Because the double bed still has the foisty, unwashed navy duvet cover and pillow slips on, I said I'd sleep on the couch. Granville in single bed upstairs. Had to lie doubled up all night, and could smell the foisty stench from where the bathroom floor has been dug up. Hardly slept at all.

CHRISTMAS DAY

Sunny and mild. Granville and I went for a walk after we'd opened presents. Had a sharp pain in my left side all the time. Wore the black and white scarf Audrey sent me. Awful going back into dark cottage while still sunny. Electric lights on all the time. Turkey – didn't eat much of that – and vegetables for lunch. Drank water instead of wine. Didn't feel well.

Afternoon. All of us went for the same walk up Terrys Lane. Alan peering through hedges all the time, trying to see if he could see his own cottage. Not much point in leaving it. He has no conversation whatsoever. Wore his usual brown suede coat. Cold shivers running down my back. Caroline and I wanted to go to the toilet, and asked Alan – who was way behind trying to locate his house – to hurry with the door keys. But he loitered behind more than ever. Why not give us the keys?

Finally inside, he played a loud pop tape, and my head felt heavy. I didn't have any tea or supper. Went into the small bedroom about 9 p.m. and stayed there. Could hear Alan telling the same dreary tale on the telephone. First to his mother, his grandma, and his brother. Bedroom cluttered up. He's so cocky in his attitude, and obviously uneducated.

BOXING DAY

Alan driving Caroline's car to 29 Springdale Drive. Had to take our shoes off before allowed in. Bit like entering a mosque. Everybody did, except Alan. Anne and Andrew were leaving as we arrived. We'd been expected earlier but Alan never gets a move on.

Clockwise from
top left: Jack Sykes,
Hazel, Hilda, Annie,
Rena Sykes, Robert
and Granville. 1987

Buffet lunch, and the Christmas cake I'd made. Alan said there wasn't enough light in the room when I was taking photographs. He insisted: 'I know what I am talking about.' Going on and on about it. I retorted that I'd been publishing photographs with it for the past umpteen years, and even Robert told him I've taken some good pictures with it. Alan, who knows nothing, not even what 'faux pas' means. It was mentioned on TV and he didn't know what it meant. Trying to be an authority on photography. I wished him far away.

Then he wanted to look at the camera, and started playing about with it. Worse, the cat that used to live where Elizabeth and Robert now are has been abandoned. Alan kept trying to capture it and administer a tranquilizer, so he could adorn the cottage with the old-fashioned-looking tabby cat.

Eventually it came in for some turkey and was put in the wicker hamper basket. It mewed a few times on the motorway back to Alan's cottage. I've named the cat Christmas. Not appropriate calling 'Come in, Christmas' I suppose, in a heat wave, but it fitted better than any other name.

SUNDAY 27 DECEMBER
G. and I stayed in Caroline's flat last night. It was raining, mild and dull as we read *The Sunday Times*, expecting to be driven to Alan's parents for a meal. Throat aching, due to those fumes. Alan had said we'd to be ready for 2 p.m. Always imagine the worst when people aren't on time – it was 2.45 p.m. when they finally arrived. No apologies.

I asked about the cat. When he is out at work all day, Christmas would miss fresh air, and be breathing in fumes from the damp bathroom. 'Don't be daft,' he snarled, '*you* are the only one who's affected.'

By that time I was in the back of the car with Granville and his remark was like a match to a tinderbox. '*You're* daft,' I spat back.

'Are we going?' asked Caroline.

'No, we aren't,' Granville replied, getting out of the car. We went back to the flat. An utter farce, bathing, changing, and putting make-up on, to stay there.

Came out again. In Beauty to Uxbridge. What a dead place when shops are shut. Only layabouts and queer types smoking and squatting on pavements. Back to flat. Made vegetarian sausages and eggs for tea.

The day was saved by an excellent film on TV, *Mary Rose*. A girl who disappeared on a remote island. Found twenty-five years later, exactly the same as when she was lost.

Walking Bowlegged
into the 1990s

CHRISTMAS EVE

Windy and dull. Left home 9.30 a.m. Arrived at Forge Cottage, Upper Wardington, Oxfordshire, at about noon. Christmas the cat was hiding beneath the bed. Caroline had made a quiche for lunch. In car to Prospect House, Oxford Road, Banbury. Going to have bed and breakfast there. Back to Alan's cottage then for a walk. Evening. In pouring rain, in Alan's car, to Oxford Cottage, Lower Wardington, to join in with the carols. A band played and we had mulled wine. Back to Alan's, listened to radio, left about 9 p.m. so that he and Caroline could sprawl on the bed. Only four hard seats and no cushions. I had made one for the cat – almost wished I'd kept it for us four to swap around to sit on.

The band was the Hook Norton Silver Band. Had a vile shower on our return – no bath in room. Don't know how to work the thing and hated standing up instead of luxuriating lying down. One hard bath towel of limited size for two. Only the owners Tony and Stella Amos in the lounge to talk with.

CHRISTMAS DAY

Breakfast with well-to-do Polish lady. Her daughter and family have a country cottage. Not enough room for her to sleep there, either. Her daughter speaks nine languages.

To Alan's cottage. Fine and sunny in afternoon. All four to Wardington Church. Not many there. Back to Alan's. Slice of turkey, nut roast (I don't eat meat if I can avoid it), potatoes and hard parsnips. Not cooked enough. To avoid being mushy, I suppose. Puddings I had taken. Enjoyed it all.

Exchanged presents. Alan gave us none. A car ice scraper for Caroline and a £5.95 vegetarian cookery book. I felt upset that Caroline had given him a shirt, a

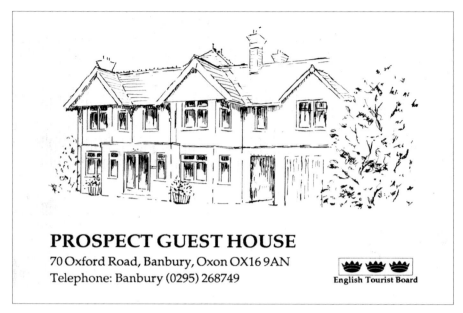

PROSPECT GUEST HOUSE

70 Oxford Road, Banbury, Oxon OX16 9AN
Telephone: Banbury (0295) 268749

English Tourist Board

'Stella and Tony Amos offer you their personal attention and comfortable refurbished accommodation.'

big hardback antiques book, a radio with headphones, and other presents. Went for a walk. Back to open last of the presents. After tea listened to radio. Very uncomfortable on hard-backed seats. Hour after hour.

Granville drove on the unlit country lanes to guesthouse in Banbury. To bed to rest and watch TV. I never know how to put TVs on in strange places, so glad Granville was there.

(Christmas, the cat, had been down to its litter tray in the tiny entrance to Alan's cottage when we arrived. Alan simply covered it up with special stuff – said it would 'absorb it'. Thought it would have been emptied outside. Laughable – and an old-fashioned Christmassy atmosphere. If anyone loves animals as we do, they are alright.)

BOXING DAY
Sunny. Talking with Mrs Flashner of Ealing, and the couple from St Anne's at breakfast. When we arrived at Forge Cottage, Alan was hunched over the coal fire drinking coffee. Christmas the cat still either sulking or heavily depressed under the bed. An enjoyable walk – except for Alan insisting that certain hedging looked as it did because 'trees grow sideways'. He'd been 'reading books about it'. I found in a disused cottage a plastic bag and gathered wood. He didn't wear the gloves sent by Elizabeth. Pushed his hands in his pockets instead. Yesterday, at about 4 p.m., Ceauçescu and his wife were shot dead in Romania after a brief trial.

WEDNESDAY 27 DECEMBER

Dull. Caroline working in Bromley. I bought black trench-style raincoat at Alders. Reduced to £49.95. Met Caroline at 12 noon. Bought her one. Debenhams for sandwiches, cakes and coffee. Wore blue hand-knitted suit. On M25, opposite side, a forty-foot lorry had overturned. Hold-up on return journey as well. Caroline made a detour through Esher and Twickenham.

At the flat she had a quick change and went to Alan's parents for a meal. We had a packet of lasagne I'd taken, and ice cream. We watched TV. I'd sent a box of table mats for Alan's mother, a pack of soap for his grandma. From Marks and Spencer.

When Caroline came back she gave me a pack of Marks and Spencer small soaps and a small packet of chocolates for Granville from Alan's mother. Granville bought a grey suede jacket in Dunn's outfitters this morning.

THURSDAY 28 DECEMBER

Fine but dull. To Eastbourne with Caroline. In Laura Ashley's establishment a boy was screaming piercingly. 'Swine,' I muttered to Caroline.

'That happens to be my son!' a hoity-toity-voiced woman reproved.

'Well, it's an awful noise,' I said.

'Good for you,' another customer praised, patting me on the back.

Caroline bought a red patterned blouse. Fish and chips for lunch in Debenhams. Fed pigeons earlier. Bought blue skirt, and one for Caroline. £14 each. Tartan skirt, £17.95. Man's cardigan £7.69, for Robert when we go there tomorrow. Back to Caroline's. All watching *Gone with the Wind*.

FRIDAY 29 DECEMBER

Ages packing car. Caroline to work. We went to Ashford. Grey, sunless day. When we arrived at Elizabeth's only Max, Molly's dog, greeted us. Robert stayed in the kitchen. So did Abigail. Not exactly a cordial welcome. The twins eventually came in and ran back. Elizabeth upstairs changing bedclothes. Didn't even shout down to us. Nowhere to put our clothes or take our cases. Nobody showed us where we would sleep. Abigail, Charlotte and Adele never mentioned the berets and scarves, nor did they find them when I asked to see what they looked like on them. I'd spent a lot of time knitting them.

Then Abigail plonked hers in an ungainly manner on her head, snatched it off, and stuffed it into a box. No 'thank you' or anything. Felt sick. 'Pop' blaring in living room, water gushing out of taps. Max, outside, unhappily gazing in while we had cheese, pickles and bread for lunch. Felt like eating mine outside with Max too.

Elizabeth went to the shops. Max was lying beneath the table. 'Max,' thundered Robert's bad-tempered voice – and the poor dog wondered what he'd done wrong again. His tail drooped. I wanted to cry. One of the twins had already been sent

A Christmas postcard from Hazel's collection (VI).

upstairs for doing something wrong. Then they demanded a 'real' Christmas drink. Molly, Robert's mother, kept blowing her nose and coughing, and gave them one from her glass of sherry. Then I asked Robert to try the cardigan on we'd bought the previous day. 'I only wear suits,' he snarled, chucking it back to me. I re-wrapped it, along with the pictures they'd rejected, and put them back in the car. Then I took Max out to get away from such rude, uncivilized people. The children were out on skates. Earlier, gave Elizabeth a set of different honeys in jars. 'We've already got some,' she said.

As I was going out, Robert sarcastically called, 'Do you want a cap? We've more knitted ones here than we can deal with.' And because Adele had picked a toffee from the floor and put it in her mouth, Robert screamed at poor Max, who was lying quietly in the main room. Cowed, he immediately slunk to Robert. How could I stay after that? His mother was boasting about once drinking nine glasses of port – *not* the kind of atmosphere I feel comfortable in.

Told Granville I couldn't stay there any longer. They began playing Scrabble when we returned, but I felt choked with dismay.

Everything was already back in our car. If Elizabeth had been there a scene would have blown up. She never blames those who are to blame. Wished we could have rescued Max from such an environment as we left without saying goodbye. Granville drove back to Caroline's – where only hours before we had left with the two red cases, leaving the flat with more space. She was watching *Gone with the Wind* in her dressing gown, not expecting to see us again so soon. Had grilled mushrooms and tomatoes with her, than Granville drove all the way home to Yorkshire. Arriving after midnight. House icy cold, so was the bed. But heaven to be away from that horrible atmosphere in Ashford.

How true: it is the welcome that matters, not the presents. A warm welcome preferable to all the wealth in the world.

SATURDAY 30 DECEMBER

Dull, grey. Shopping in town. Home for lunch. Elizabeth 'phoned. G. answered. 'What do you think you're playing at?' she screamed. 'You will never see me or the children again.' She slammed the 'phone down and the receiver must have been taken off the hook. I wrote a letter, telling her why. Surely she would have known, had she not been at the shops, when Robert shouted so violently at poor Max – and water wasting – and no 'thank you' for any presents etc. As Rhett Butler said in *Gone with the Wind*, unless and until you all have more manners, 'Frankly, I (we) don't give a damn.' The only regret is that she has turned out so differently to how she was brought up.

One doesn't require money to have good manners. Which she always had before submerging herself with 'pop' and the Connolly culture, and estranging herself from us. I knew when she first met him this would be the result. Robert's auntie Eileen telephoned. She has bought my book and how fascinating she finds it. Elizabeth has made no comment about the book. Last night so upset didn't notice the car door was open on the way back as far as Northamptonshire! Kept thinking there was a draught. But needed it to cool down I suppose.

NEW YEAR'S EVE

Dull. Finished letter to Elizabeth. Wrote to Alan telling him Granville is now walking bowlegged into the 1990s after falling – and may Alan's trees always grow sideways (that argument he and Granville had on the country walk).

Granville put on grey overcoat and new grey jerkin. No coloured scarf or anything. He looked like a dead mouse. In Beauty to Eileen and Ronnie Pogson's at Kirkheaton to sign a book.

Raining, grey, misty. Eileen said the least anyone can do is to say 'thank you' (Elizabeth and family). Home for tea. Leeks, mashed potato, and grated cheese baked in oven. Oranges, bananas and honey, custard.

Evening. Knitting green dress. Watching Clive James' review of the '80s on TV. Not half as good as usual. No scenes of people in Trafalgar Square.

Didn't kiss Granville at midnight because it's so contrived. And artificial doing what one is expected to do.

In future I'll spend my time knitting for myself. Remembered on Christmas Day in Romania the president and his wife facing a firing squad at 4 p.m. For all the months of ridiculous false build-up to the so-called festive season, it frequently heralds not the angels singing, but families squabbling. And those whose fault it is refuse to take their blinkers off and lay the blame where it belongs.

1990

Horrible Soggy Bits

SUNDAY 23 DECEMBER

Evening to Kirkheaton Church. Granville and Beauty were stuck in the mud. When they surged forward it was like mud fireworks in the headlights. Wish we hadn't gone. No choirboys, guitars and screens with words on, sung in a monotone. Horrible.

Then they started clapping. I said loudly it was just like Butlin's, so those nearby could hear. Then depressing images of deprived coloured people were shown, alongside those of affluent, car-owning white people. Another group of people with silly painted white faces and white gloves ranted on about what hands do. Bored stiff and feeling slightly queasy, what with the wine this lunchtime then the mud fireworks. Came out after the collection, when they began the same monotonous non-carols again on the screens.

Told the chap at the door, 'It's just like Butlin's – no wonder people stop going to church.'

My walking out of places at Christmas time is becoming more of a tradition than the carols. Didn't have any tea when back home.

Granville and Caroline did. Letter from Meg Francis this morning. Her husband is learning the piano for when he retires. Another of her friends plays bridge (wouldn't want that). Another writes. Another was a consultant, now retired.

What, though, will Granville fill his days with?

CHRISTMAS EVE

Winnie here for tea. Beautiful clear blue sky and sunshine. Caroline dusted Welsh dresser and I tidied up while listening to carols and poetry reading on radio.

Afternoon. Granville and Caroline took some fresh salmon for his sister Margaret at Golcar. Then collected Dorothy from Oak Avenue and Winnie. Don't

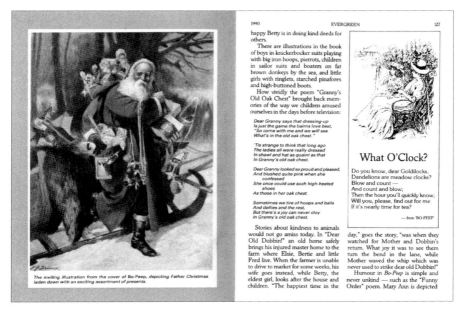

1990   EVERGREEN   127

happy Betty is in doing kind deeds for others.

There are illustrations in the book of boys in knickerbocker suits playing with big iron hoops, pierrots, children in sailor suits and boaters on fat brown donkeys by the sea, and little girls with ringlets, starched pinafores and high-buttoned boots.

How vividly the poem "Granny's Old Oak Chest" brought back memories of the way we children amused ourselves in the days before television:

*Dear Granny says that dressing-up
Is just the game the bairns love best,
"So come with me and we will see
What's in the old oak chest."*

*'Tis strange to think that long ago
The ladies all were really dressed
In shawl and hat as quaint as that
In Granny's old oak chest.*

*Dear Granny looked so proud and pleased,
And blushed quite pink when she
confessed
She once could use such high-heeled
shoes
As those in her oak chest.*

*Sometimes we tire of hoops and balls
And dollies and the rest,
But there's a joy we can never cloy
In Granny's old oak chest.*

Stories about kindness to animals would not go amiss today. In "Dear Old Dobbin!" an old horse safely brings his injured master home to the farm where Elsie, Bertie and little Fred live. When the farmer is unable to drive to market for some weeks, his wife goes instead, while Betty, the eldest girl, looks after the house and children. "The happiest time in the

What O'Clock?

Do you know, dear Goldilocks,
Dandelions are meadow clocks?
Blow and count —
And count and blow;
Then the hour you'll quickly know;
Will you, please, find out for me
If it's nearly time for tea?

— from 'BO-PEEP'

day," goes the story, "was when they watched for Mother and Dobbin's return. What joy it was to see them turn the bend in the lane, while Mother waved the whip which was never used to strike dear old Dobbin!"

Humour in *Bo-Peep* is simple and never unkind — such as the "Funny Order" poem. Mary Ann is depicted

The inviting illustration from the cover of Bo-Peep, depicting Father Christmas laden down with an exciting assortment of presents.

Hazel writes about Bo-Peep for the Winter 1990/91 issue of *Evergreen*, 'Britain's Brightest Country Quarterly'.

like old people being on their own at Christmas when we can help give them a happy one. We gave Winnie a copy of my book, also one of *Evergreen*. She gave us an *Examiner* calendar! Dorothy, who has already given us a big tin of biscuits, handed us a bottle of non-alcoholic wine too. I put King's College carols on – thinking Winnie would want to hear them. She didn't. I spent most of the afternoon cooking. Plaice, vegetables. Had prepared jelly and tangerines etc. before.

After tea in Beauty to service at Holy Trinity Church. It started at 7.30 p.m. Winnie talking in a loud whisper about the candles to Dorothy. Caroline laughing, trying not to let anyone see she was. I asked Dorothy if she had a tissue for Granville – she didn't hear properly so I repeated 'a tissue, a tissue,' which sounded as though I was sneezing. Making Caroline and me giggle more than ever.

We drove Winnie home, then Dorothy back to Golcar. Played carols from the Chapter House, York, on radio when in bed. Granville wanted the door closed so he could go to sleep. To avoid his Christmas snores I was in the other bedroom.

We all had our stockings full of presents at the sides of our beds while we slept. Like three guard dogs.

CHRISTMAS DAY

Torrential rain and windy. In Beauty to Dalton St Paul's. It was just finishing as we crept inside. Blown out again into wind and rain. To Trinity Church for the service. Home for lunch after calling to see ninety-three-year-old Mary Taylor, in the nursing home next door. She used to be a piano teacher, and had dozens of knitted slippers outside the main room for pupils to change into from outdoor shoes.

Salad, coffee etc. Opening our presents with Caroline. Then I made nut roast and vegetables, Christmas pudding and all the usual before going to Betty and Norman's at 15 Newlands Avenue, Birkby. Caroline wore the black velvet dress I gave her. We sat in back room talking with Betty while Granville was in the front one with Norman. To be polite – Norman wanted to watch *Coronation Street*.

We didn't. How boring! Betty had promised if we went she'd make sure that Shay, the short-tempered dog, was kept away from where we were. When we went into the front room for a buffet supper, Shay shot in as well, darting beneath Granville's chair. On her Christmas card she had promised faithfully she'd make sure it didn't get near him. Known to be a biter. He sat absolutely still, but petrified-looking. Shay's face – and teeth – right behind his ankles. And the leg he had a blood clot in had been bleeding today. Eventually Shay was grabbed and returned to the back room. With the promise that he'd be able to bark to the Hoover after we'd gone.

Betty and Shay, Christmas Day 1990.

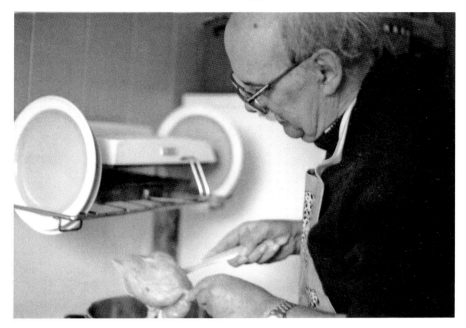

'One man's retirement – happiness is making marmalade!'

Norman has solved the question of how to fill his redundant days and retirement years. He redecorates the house non-stop. No sooner one room done, he begins again. On another. On the hallway wall was a big warning sign, 'BEWARE OF WET PAINT'. And Shay is white.

How could we enjoy the delicious buffet, never knowing when Shay would strike? On edge as usual.

BOXING DAY

No Shay drawing blood for Granville to worry about today. Rain and wind again. Granville and Caroline took a white dish filled with biscuits and two grapefruits for mother's friend Mrs Ellison, up the fields. I prepared lunch, including Christmas pudding and white sauce. Enjoy catering for those whom I enjoy being with.

Afternoon. Made two jars of lemon cheese for Caroline to take back, also a chocolate cake. She was reading Victorian magazines and old books, and my diaries. Caroline is easy to entertain. Give her old books and she is happy, cosy in front of a blazing fire.

Granville read the Sherlock Holmes book, one of his presents from Caroline. Salad for tea. Caroline enjoyed hers on a tray by the fire. Hate it when she has to go back to a flat with no proper fire.

Granville wanted to wash up. He plunged everything – including bits of nut roast and other food – into the bowl then poured washing up liquid – tons of it

– into the lot. We jostled at the sink, but I won, making him leave it for me to do if he doesn't know that plates must first be rinsed.

It's alright people advising, 'You must let him wash up and do things.' But how can I when he uses almost a whole bottle of detergent every time – and then they're still stuck up with horrible soggy bits all over. He's best at making marmalade. But can't do that every month of the year.

They watched TV in the evening and a horror film.

THURSDAY 27 DECEMBER

Not as dull as yesterday, but windy and sleet in the wind. Occasional sunshine. Granville and Caroline across to Oaklands to gather wood while I prepared early lunch. Cheese and onion pie, leek and mushroom sauce, ground rice pudding and chopped dates. Washed car for Caroline.

She packed belongings into it. Nearly cry when the car disappears and the sound of her final 'toot' – then exasperation. She left after midday, leaving her grey boots behind. All afternoon clearing up and wishing Caroline lived nearer, and had a proper house and fire.

New fruit bush in garden was leaning over, but Granville wouldn't go out and tie it up. And he constantly turns the sound down on TV before a programme is finished. So he can't hear the adverts, and then it's too low to hear the beginning of a programme we want to watch.

The morning began with Granville losing his wallet, and everything in it. Caroline, whose car was nearer the house – behind Beauty in the drive – said she wouldn't be able to get her car out if he couldn't find his keys.

A lifetime of this kind of thing is quite unthinkable. Losing his spectacles every other minute is bad enough. Caroline found the keys in the old green jacket he wore yesterday. And I'd made lunch early so she could avoid heavy traffic later in the day.

FRIDAY 28 DECEMBER

Big black feet marks on bath where Granville had been last night. Up later than next door – who routinely go to town. Upset if we are getting into 'old age' ways already. Granville to Lodge's for vegetables and pickling vinegar. Torrential rain, but went for walk to Almondbury village. One child in rainhood and mac deliberately stood beneath an overflow pipe for the fun of having the water banging on to her head. Never been as soaked for years. Had to take all our outer – and some inner – clothes off when home. But good fun – and a glorious fire to dry ourselves out on our return.

SATURDAY 29 DECEMBER

Almost worth the vexations of some parts of Christmas when it's over and we are free again to do what we want. And for letters to resume dropping through letterbox. Letter from Shirley – Philip's daughter. Didn't realise I'd had two books published – she was pleased to see her picture in one! Makes her feel old to be 'part of history' though. Toby the dog and Shirley had their photographs in the weekly Yarmouth paper – captioned 'lonely figure walking the dog'. When it probably meant 'there's always some prat out whatever the weather'. Toby was starstruck for some time afterwards! Shirley went to a fancy dress from work on Christmas Eve. One friend went as a St Trinian's schoolgirl, and looked like Billy Bunter in drag. Shirley has done a sponsored swim for orphaned pussy cats, raising over £70. Sorry to hear Granville has lost his job. 'All the best for the New Year. Love, Shirley, John and Toby.'

Our usual after-Christmas treat – in Beauty, arriving Leeds before 9 a.m. for the sales. Traffic wardens advised not leaving Beauty where we had done. Football supporters' buses starting from there at lunchtime, drunks may damage the car. Bought cream blouse at Laura Ashley, £9. Hand towels reduced to £1.99 at Rackham's. Prawn salads, £2.20 each, in Lewis'. When Granville was returning from the counter with two coffees on a tray, 50p each, he leaned back to grab more sugars and black pepper sachets and the tray listed as though on the High Seas. I ran from the table to take it from him. We enjoy the haul of free sachets, especially the black peppers pushed into my handbag. More coffee when home, and Christmas cake and cheese.

Evening. Read *The Times* and watched *Blind Date*. I've put part of my money from Alliance & Leicester, withdrawn this morning, towards buying a Marks and Spencer reading lamp. They were reduced to £25. Wouldn't want to go to Leeds sales with anybody else but Granville!

SUNDAY 30 DECEMBER

Often it feels more like Christmas should do before and after it is over. Cold and dry this morning. Granville did the washing after making breakfast – grapefruit cut the wrong way, had to scoop it out lengthways. A sheet came off the line, tangling over Shaw's fence and one of their bushes. Pulled all blankets out of cupboard and washed it out. Don't know how people manage in a flat with no storage space or garden. Must be Hell.

Afternoon. In Beauty to Almondbury, parking by field while we gathered firewood. I broke some chestnut twigs, with buds, fat and sticky, to put into vase when we got home. Salad, coffee, Christmas cake and Norfolk Punch. Changed into red coat and black beret to walk back up to Almondbury Church for a carol service beginning at 4.15 p.m.

Wish Caroline had been there – a proper choir, dressed in surplus, vicar, traditional carols and readings. Found 10p by a hassock.

A party afterwards for those who wished to stay in the church hall. The old and lonely. But we wanted to get a fire going at home. Walked back. More Christmas spirit than the other days. Tea at 6.20 p.m.

Read part of *The Sunday Times* by a beautiful fire scented with wood we gathered this afternoon. In back bedroom at first with Granville, until he started deep snoring. Moonlight bright in front bedroom.

NEW YEAR'S EVE

Granville to town to pay bills and discuss money at the Alliance. I continued clearing up then wrote to publisher Alan Sutton. Typed a letter to *Woman's Realm*. Husband cut grapefruit lengthways. What to do? Not with the drunken sailor, but with the redundant shipping manager?

Lunch at home with Granville. Then Audrey telephoned. For nearly two hours. Not bothered about money – Philip died when a bank manager, no financial worries. But hates her life alone, except for the dog.

Drizzling rain as we went in Beauty to take cat Christmas stockings to Tom and Muriel Jessop's cats at Deighton.

Trixie was on top of the television, but came down and ate some dried fish bits. Poor old Sooty, bemused, went out. John Hall was there. Shop assistant at our shop before dad died in 1948. Still lives happily in same house and district. They seemed surprised that Granville only gets £9,000 redundancy, then another £10,000 for the rest of our lives. Unless either of us earns extra.

Muriel made coffee and we had some cake and talked about days gone by. Gave her a box of chocolates and some colour photographs I'd taken earlier in the year. Left about 5 p.m. to come home for tea. I made Welsh rarebit, eaten in firelight – best part of Christmas when it's over. Caroline 'phoned. Going out with friends this evening.

Granville and I watched an opera on TV. The final appearance of Joan Sutherland, soprano. She wore a massively ornate green ballgown – so large that Pavarotti could barely get near enough to sing with her. Stayed up till just after midnight.

Don't know yet whether I'm looking forward to 1991 or not. All depends on how Granville reacts to not going out to work.

1993

Psycho

THURSDAY 23 DECEMBER

Elizabeth and children arrived at about 1.30 p.m. Genine and her children brought presents for them. Caroline arrived about 3 p.m. Middle bedroom a minefield of presents. Donald Parkinson brought presents. Lesley stayed in car so her hair wouldn't get wet. Charlotte read *Granny's Wonderful Chair* (part of it), a prize won by my mother when a girl in Boroughbridge. A Sunday School award. Granville and Abigail played Auctions after lunch.

CHRISTMAS EVE

Bright, sunny. Usual walk, Thurstonland and Stocksmoor. Called at Joan and Harold's for coffee and mince pies. Abigail had that aloof, sulky look and not talking. Salad lunch at home.

Afternoon. Gave Caroline her presents in a pillow slip as will never have time to look at everything tomorrow. Didn't know what they would like for tea – maybe vegetarian burgers? Naturally, uproar with Adele and Charlotte. And couldn't cook them properly altogether, as not enough room in oven. Then Elizabeth mistakenly thought I'd said we'd have some left in the fridge. Granville ate them reluctantly, as I'd had enough. Elizabeth made beans and chips for the twins who complained about those also. E. went to buy milk. They only have a certain kind. She said one of the games she bought for them is called 'Psycho'.

Played games until time to go in Caroline's car to Almondbury Church. Abigail tired, lolled her head on my shoulder all the time. I sat between her and Charlotte. Adele started to cry when the choir sang without congregation joining – she wanted to sing as well. Yet if asked to sing, she refuses.

A letter I have from Caroline in diary about the grandchildren:

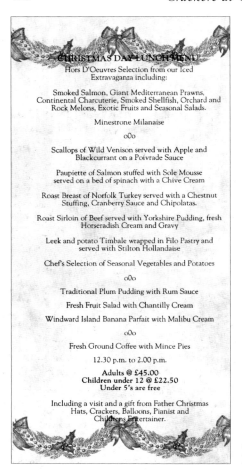

Christmas Day lunch menu at the Hilton, 1993.

Dear both,

Enclosed a few envelopes, all I've got at the moment. Forgot to tell you what happened that was funny at Liz's. Abigail had drawn up a rota for everyone to do a job. On the Sunday morning it was Charlotte's job to make drinks and put milk in people's tea. She was still in bed when Abigail went to make herself a cup of tea and tried to get the milk out of the fridge – Adele blocked it with her body and arms, said she couldn't get the milk as it was Charlotte's job. There was a full scale row then as Abigail wanted her tea *then*. Adele shouted up to Charlotte, who came bounding down to get the milk and pour it in the cup! It was nearly lunchtime even then.

I'm enrolling for an evening class in psychology – get a diploma at the end if I pass the exam. See you soon.

Love C.

XXXXXXX

CHRISTMAS DAY

4.30 a.m. Twins awake downstairs. Standing with backs to each other so they wouldn't see what the other was opening. Everything alright until they got to pairs of socks – one heel was blue, the other green. One started crying, wanting to swap them. Granville got in bed with them as referee.

Fine morning, occasional snow flurries. I wore black skirt, green frilled blouse to go to the Hilton Hotel at Ainley Top. I sat next to Elizabeth. Charlotte and Adele opposite. Abigail and Granville together. They didn't want soup, so went to choose hors d'œuvre. There was everything imaginable – yet all three walked round the enormous display, an ice sculpture at the centre, and returned scowling. There was nothing they liked! Crying because they couldn't have tinned tomato soup. I said how 'disgusting' (their non-stop word) they were. Pulled face at Adele – who, one would have thought, had been badly done to. When she pulled a face at me, I nudged Elizabeth, pointing at her daughter. No response. Then Abigail glared in a foul manner at me so I said, 'And don't you glare like that either.'

More tears. No apple sauce with the turkey, only cranberry and everything else. A small boy who cracked his mother across her face allowed to get away with it – £45 adults, £22 for each child. I've seen better manners in a pig sty.

Then Father Christmas arrived to great applause. Secretly I'd have cheered the arrival of Pierrepont the hangman. Twins received a selection box each, also a Barbie doll. Abigail a geometry set and selection box. Home about 3.30 p.m. Ages everyone opening presents. Couldn't hear carols on radio, first year didn't hear

Adele. Christmas at the Hilton, 1993.

the Queen's speech. All those three are interested in is riving open more and more presents.

What a wasted day. When the meal was over, a Mongol-type little girl grabbed a salt cellar and went round pouring salt into cups, over tables, milk jugs, over the floor. A waiter tried to take it from her. Last seen scampering down the ramp with it. (I didn't know there were steps, and almost skidded down the ramp meant for wheelchairs.)

Granville kept eating more to make up for what Abigail, Adele and Charlotte didn't have. Wrapped some turkey up to bring back for a cat.

BOXING DAY

White frost, brilliant sunshine. Couldn't see it in living room – security shutters wouldn't go up yet again. Geoff Turner came and put logs of wood beneath bottom of shutters to enable a glimmer of light to get in. All this wasted electric light when so bright outside – Granville put telephone messages on answering machines, those of Cordula – who never responded the last time shutters wouldn't go up – and a firm who came about three weeks ago. Repair bill was £35. Cordula need drumming out of business the way they ignore customers once they have their money.

Walk with Edith after sandwiches, coffee and Christmas cake in front room. She didn't stay for tea in case her car froze up.

After ours (Elizabeth and children had gone to Molly's at Bradley, where Robert and all his family were) we watched *Keeping Up Appearances* and *One Foot in the Grave*.

What a fiasco having to fiddle around with coffee tables when the meal could have been set out in the living room. Blasted shutters – or rather the firm who will not put them right once and for all. Most of the Christmas decorations are in the living room as well.

MONDAY 27 DECEMBER

Sunny. Awful not being able to see out of living room window, and awake in early hours thinking how Elizabeth said she liked Sue Townsend's skit on the royal family, *Hell Close* or something. But she hasn't even read mine yet, which she has had for a few weeks. Also the fiasco and awful behaviour of her children at the Hilton Hotel has never been referred to again. She shouts at *me*, but never at the instigators of disharmony. If children were brought up to behave properly there wouldn't be the so called 'generation gap'.

To Leeds with Granville. To Rackhams. The chair they delivered not the same as the one we ordered. Suggested knocking £30 off – I said how about inconvenience? He will telephone tomorrow. To Pudsey Book Fair. Bought a book I think my mother was reading when expecting me. She had said how she'd read a book and thought the name Hazel was lovely. It is called *What Hazel Did*, priced at £10, but Granville bartered dealer down to £7.50. Also *Anderson's Stories*, £2.50, and *The Royal Annual* for £1. Enjoyed it far more than Christmas.

Called at Reedman's warehouse. Elizabeth went to tea at Molly's. When she returned, Adele and Charlotte were sent straight to bed. They had been 'carrying on' most of the time. Abigail looked terribly sad. I almost started to cry; so did she. I brought drawing pencils and sketch pads down and she enjoyed that. Caroline read my book. I talked with Abigail until 11.30 p.m. then she went onto the air bed, which has been blown up. If children were talked to more, instead of non-stop television, they'd be far happier and well-behaved.

TUESDAY 28 DECEMBER

Snowing. Granville sat by telephone ringing various places about the shutters. Finally ringing the police to enquire if *they* knew anyone who could remove, or repair, the shutters. They didn't. Granville had a nail stuck inside his trousers – to make his limp more authentic. Brian Hulme called. Cake and coffee in front room. Granville parking on Wood Street. Couldn't open door – Caroline leapt out of passenger seat when he called me 'a neurotic bitch' and I pulled his black cap off and thumped his shoulder.

5 p.m. Rackhams 'phoned again about the chair. Now saying it's the same as the one on shop floor that we ordered. Bringing it on Thursday to compare them. It definitely isn't.

WEDNESDAY 29 DECEMBER

Twins still in bed at 11 a.m. Couldn't light a fire in there with sofa bed out. Abigail arrived downstairs in Granville's dressing gown. Refused breakfast, then went rooting around among her presents for a tiny pot of strawberry jam. The twins refused *anything* suggested. Maddening when Abigail said 'at Grandma Molly's we had bacon, mushrooms, sausages, tomatoes' – as though marvellous there, yet at the best hotel there was nothing they fancied.

The most irritating children we have ever met. Then the twins wanted the pom-pons cutting off the pink and blue mohair jumpers I've knitted for them.

They went to stay at friends in Bradley Lane. Leaving the knitted caps here. Refused to wear the red corduroy trousers we have bought for them also. What bad manners! Can't believe Elizabeth allows them to be like this. Life would be a lot easier for her if she insisted on good behaviour, instead of letting them get away with such boorish ways.

Man from Cordula Shutters arrived after they'd gone. Said they hadn't been installed correctly in the first place. He was ages. Kitchen window open for electric plug to be on, letting cold air in. Still blacked out in living room, so he had coffee in front room. He agreed what an awful carry-on it has been. First daylight came in living room – then down the blackness came again. We all screamed. It was like being in a horror film! Gave him a letter for Cordula saying how distressed everyone had been, and if they failed to suggest compensation for spoiling

Christmas – because they hadn't put the matter right on 2 December – we will take the matter further.

The 'light of the world' has not been born at 58 Greenhead Lane at Christmas.

NEW YEAR'S EVE

Drew £900 from Alliance & Leicester, transferred it to Lloyds to pay off Christmas expenses. Signed books in a shop. Bought a few tins of tomato soup. In case Adele and Charlotte want some on Sunday. Of course, now we have some they won't like it anymore. A black woman has given birth to a white baby after treatment by a fertility clinic. What an idiotic world. Who needs *crackers* at Christmas?

Delighted an article I sent to the *Huddersfield Examiner*, denouncing 'pop' Michael Jackson and co. has been published. Best way I can think of to end a year. What use is it having an opinion if you keep it to yourself! Controversy is preferable to being a bore. Those who piously murmur, 'Oh, I can't say that!' – why? Took shopping home then to Cowlersley with a cat's Christmas stocking for Marion and Brian's. Wish all the cats, dogs and other animals in the world could have a Christmas stocking and happiness. Returned the airbed.

Evening. Caroline telephoned. Was sick after being to a pub for a meal in Crewe yesterday. Only eaten a banana all day.

Wonder if somebody could collate all the telephone conversations at Christmas, would it make a bestseller? Herman Sanderson 'phoned to congratulate me on the article in the *Examiner*. He thinks the same as I do – and plays the organ at Leeds Road Spiritualist Church. Asked if we'd like to go to the New Year's Eve party there. But there was a big log on the fire, opera on radio, and ballads. Besides, don't want to risk being out at midnight when drunkards may be about. And if the log fell out onto the rug, we certainly wouldn't have a Happy New Year.

Besides, I like to look back in old diaries after guests have departed and we can relax by ourselves. Read a letter dated 2 November 1993, from Bheil Land Associates Ltd. Literary, theatre, and film agents.

Dear Ms Wheeler,
   Thank you for your letter dated 27 October. I'm sorry you find Adrian Mole a bore, and, as Sue Townsend's agent, obviously it's unlikely that I'd find your writing more inspiring. I'm sorry.
   Yours sincerely,
   Giles Gordon.

On reflection, perhaps it may be wiser not to say what you think sometimes – but I can't help it.

INTERLUDE

Christmas Diversions

Why pay enormous sums to take one's family away for Christmas when the merriest times (before the Second World War) were those spent at home? Without television. Some say, 'Oh, but children are different today – they wouldn't enjoy the simple things we did.' How wrong they are. Our granddaughters were worn out with museums, leisure centres, and their stomachs being churned up on expensive rides during the summer holidays.

Then they came to us, and adored playing games that we played as children. Costing nothing. I save letters and junk mail for cutting up into strips for paper and pencil games such as Consequences, General Knowledge, Country, County, Town, Bird, Fish, Animal, Fruit, Flower, Tree, Boys' and Girls' Names (all beginning with the same letter). Ten points given to a word not duplicated by other players, five if someone else has the same. Of course, small prizes can be awarded for special occasions such as Christmas or birthdays.

Abigail, eleven, and twins Adele and Charlotte, eight, had never played either of these games before. TV was completely forgotten. I've rarely seen them as animated. Competition to write the funniest 'consequence' was intense, as was thinking up unusual names. They were having to use their brains, not just sit passively watching a screen – and they loved it.

I have a book, *Games for Family Parties and Children*, given to a child for Christmas 1903. On the front are illustrations of someone's hands forming a rabbit, and another a face, shadowed in firelight against a wall. Remember the fascination of that?

After serious games requiring concentration, it's always fun to play Cat and Mouse. Clear the centre of the room and join hands to form a circle. The 'mouse', ideally a small child, is inside. A taller child plays the cat, outside. All dance round singing 'Pray, Mrs Mouse, are you within?' Mouse: 'Yes, kind sir, and I'm sitting to spin.' Puss, prowling round, has to purr, 'Miew, miew, miew.' Mouse must keep in the middle of the circle, out of the enemy's reach. But she must also frequently run in and out of it, to give Pussy a chance of catching her – and to keep the excitement high. The circle must try to defend the mouse, opening and raising their arms to admit her when she flies back into the circle, depressing their arms and drawing close together to keep out the cat. If the cat succeeds in getting into the circle the two who suffered her to do so become in their turn cat and mouse. If the mouse is caught, but the cat, when catching her, forgets to miew, it is not considered a true capture. If the mouse is caught outside the circle she pays a forfeit, and if the cat manages to touch her while in it, she also pays a forfeit.

Plenty of amusement can be afforded by the forfeits too. Activity games such as this are made more festive with carols playing in the background. Even grandparents – agile ones – will recapture the thrill of a real old-fashioned Christmas party by joining in. Indeed, if grandma begins it all by being the mouse, and grandad the cat, great hilarity will ensue.

Christmassy wrapping paper made into paper balls is ideal for the Paper Duel. Two contestants stand back to back, holding one each. Two others are their seconds. The duellists walk a few paces away from each other, turn round and try to hit their opponent with the ball. The seconds pick up the balls as they fall, then replace the duellists.

A quieter game is 'I love my love with an A'. All in a circle, one begins, 'I love my love with an A because she is amiable, I admire her because she is artless, I gave her a bouquet of azaleas.' The next person says the same three sentences but with the next letter of the alphabet, perhaps 'benevolent, beautiful, blue bells'. Each player in turn loves his or her love thus. The game is so old that James II often played 'I love my love with an A' when he was the Duke of York.

Tongue twisters used to pass many an amusing moment. Try these with grandchildren:

> Four fat friars fishing for frogs.
> Six soldiers shooting snipes.
> Seven salmon sailing in Solway.
> Ten tall tinkers taking twopence.
> Five fairies finding fireflies.
> Eleven electors eating early endive.
> Twelve tremendous tale tellers telling truth.

Children may initially say they don't want to play, but few can resist the challenge.

At a book fair we bought some old board games. In one, The New Game of Virtue Rewarded and Vice Punished, published 1818, each player has to get via the House of Correction to the House of Virtue. How to behave in a civilized manner

PIP & SQUEAK
1927 ANNUAL 1927

"MIND YOU DON'T SCORCH THE TOWEL, PIP."

Pip and Squeak's cartoon strip in the *Daily Mirror* was popular enough for a series of annuals to be spun off, from 1923 to 1939. Pip is a dog, Squeak a penguin, Wilfred, their child, a rabbit.

was largely taught through play. One board game, The Cottage of Content, or Right Roads and Wrong Ways, was published in 1848 by William Spooner of the Strand, London. Players encountered Honesty Road, Punishment Path, Lackaday Lane, Misfortune Lane and Consequence Corner. Forfeits had to be paid for frightening the frogs, and for Pride, whereas points were awarded for virtues such as Being Charitable.

Another popular game was Willy's Walk to See Grandma, published in 1869. Aero Flights was published by Chad Valley in 1910, inspired by the first successful cross-channel flight made on 25 July 1909 by Louis Bleriot from Les Boraques, near Calais, to Dover. The thirty-seven-minute crossing won him a *Daily Mail* prize of £1,000. The object of the game was to emulate Bleriot, but in the reverse direction. Trencho was a game inspired in 1917 by fighting on the Western Front. Chad Valley produced several horse-racing games: The Hunt Cup in 1910 and Grand National Steeplechase and The Stirrup Cup in 1922. They also made a range of mechanical horse games, the most successful being Escalado in 1933. Blow Football appeared in 1910, also by Chad Valley.

Aerial Attack was produced in 1942, depicting the blacked-out hours of the Blitz. Rules, rewards and punishments issued in clipped tones recalled old newsreel commentaries: 'Incendiary bomb strikes basement room, cleared according to regulations. Receive one token from other players. No. 55 – leading by light of open flame during air raid. Miss two turns for carelessness. No. 8 – dogfight in the sky. Stop to watch and miss a turn. No. 34 – enemy plane turns to escape. Go back to 28.'

Participating in any game is far superior a pastime to passively watching others enjoying themselves on a screen, especially at Christmas. Why not even have a go at inventing a new game yourself? Ban TV on Christmas Day if there are children about, and show them how to enjoy a really Merry Christmas – *and* have money at the end to buy sale items in the New Year.

But remember – have all the games programmed in advance, don't allow any child a moment's let-up to moan, 'What shall we do now, grandma?'

Having a few old annuals will help enormously too – they are full of stories, riddles, games and 'magic'. Much more for your money than anorexic modern annuals. Make going to grandma and grandad's for Christmas a treat, not a bore.

1994

Doctor Sardine

THURSDAY 17 NOVEMBER
Granville never in tip-top health, but seems to escalate going up to Christmas. Granville has a huge black mole on his head. Asked him to show me insurance policies and how I'd pay for a funeral. In early hours I stared at the clusters of black dots on the ceiling. Ordinary darkness looks like that when I'm upset. Thoughts churning round in my mind. A future with no car or husband, having to drag shopping up the lane, a garden going wild – how to deal with money? Or without it? Thought to myself, 'If a car went past, everything will be alright.' Waited till one did then into back bedroom.

Granville said he had a lot of wind – and I was almost blown back out of double bed. Immediately a bright security light flashed across the ceiling – he's always saying it's the wind that makes them go on. Laughing eased the tension somewhat. Eventually went back to my single bed, as we spread out better alone.

At 9 a.m. Granville was at the infirmary for his blood to be checked. 'Phoned to say there is a three-month waiting list and it will cost about £70 for him to be seen privately (about the mole).

SATURDAY 19 NOVEMBER
Prepared a pre-Christmas banquet for advent of another gentleman friend with Caroline. Played tape of *The Street Singer* – Arthur Tracy's 1930s romantic songs – as we ate. Nothing worse than trying to converse when wanting to eat instead. In Richard's big company car to Thurstonland for walk later. When we returned I read extracts from my 1958 and 1959 diaries for them. When Caroline was a two- then three-year-old. Showed them envelope with her two-year-old lock of hair. If there's a stack of old diaries, no necessity for any other entertainment. As long

as the diary-keeper writes the whole truth and nothing but the truth, not boring appointments.

Evening. To the Golf House by 7 p.m. for a meal. Slung my coat over a balustrade, a large wooden ball on top must have been loose and flew off, bouncing across the floor and towards diners on nearby table.

Good job it missed Granville's vulnerable balding head, which was directly in the line of fire. Slow service. Testing for suitability on Christmas Day. It's not.

Richard said he always watches a programme about a snowman on Christmas Day. No wonder Caroline kept asking Granville if we'd like a video for Christmas! But we don't. I'd hate anything to be plugged in all the time – besides, there's little enough time for writing and reading. Without gaping at even more television repeats.

Besides, we've nothing to put a video on, and certainly neither of us would be able to deal with one.

MONDAY 21 NOVEMBER

It's the warmest November since records began in 1659. Bright sunshine. Tried to hang painting of red berries I have done in the new frame. It wouldn't stay on the hook. Bloody cheapjack frames!

Afternoon. In Beauty to see Doris. The man next door whose wife died has had her ashes put in an urn on a stone near her driveway. Doris is sure she will drive over Frances one day. Gave us some frozen plums but unable to come for walk as waiting for a fridge-freezer to be delivered. Gathered twigs for the fire. Wanting to have plenty of logs in the shed for Christmas.

Evening. Caroline telephoned. Will we enquire at the Golf House if Richard's pen has been handed in? It hasn't.

WEDNESDAY 23 NOVEMBER

Letter from Caroline thanking us for a good weekend. Richard found his pen this morning tucked into his waistcoat pocket. They are going to see *A Christmas Carol* at the local theatre. She will 'get something and wrap it up from us to give R.'.

Two reviews of *Pennine People* arrived from Alan Sutton's. Washed more bookshelves in front room. Began to write a play. Then to Thurstonland – usual walk. Talked with Noel, the farmer. Lots of bulls are in the fields. One muddy white one with broad face and shoulders stared us out. Another group were knee-deep in mud, munching a stack of hay.

At least they have no worries about where to book for Christmas. 'Phoned Edith. Has lost all interest in shopping or anything now she is a widow. How terrible to feel like that.

Ada in her Santa Claus hat.
Photographed in her Elland home,
Christmas 1994.

SATURDAY 10 DECEMBER
Raining. Awoke during night thinking about Caroline and Elizabeth. And what their future will be. Tree cutters arrived across at Oaklands to cut down the lovely old tree. Photographed its demise from my writing room window. Ada telephoned from Elland to ask if we'll take tins of cat food for the one that has been abandoned. Granville to Sainsbury's. After lunch he brought a lot of the old tree across – now have big logs for Christmas. Ada greeted us wearing a red Santa Claus cap with spray of mistletoe at the front and bell at the back.

I asked Norman, after giving him a bag of butterscotch, if he had such a cap. 'No, I'm Cinderella' was the amazing humorous – for Norman – reply.

Floods and chaos in Scotland.

SUNDAY 11 DECEMBER
Fine but very windy. Geoff Turner ambled across after inspecting the fallen tree trunk and told Granville there are still a few logs. Both went across to get them.

Afternoon. Collected Doris and in Beauty to Edith's. All to Salendine Nook Baptist Church to listen to the *Messiah*. All stood for the Hallelujah chorus. Pity the pews weren't packed with people as in days gone by. It was lovely to be in a chapel as I remember them.

```
┌────────────────────────────────────────────────────────────────────┐
│                    SALENDINE NOOK BAPTIST CHURCH                     │
│                                                                      │
│           Handel's  MESSIAH   ...   ...   Sunday 11th December, 1994 │
│                                                                      │
│   Principals:                                                        │
│                                                                      │
│   Soprano    ...  Charmaine Beaumont    Tenor    ...  David Croft    │
│   Contralto  ...  Jane Hobson           Bass     ...  Kenneth Hollas │
│   Conductor  ...  Nancy Tompkins        Organist ...  George Marsden │
└────────────────────────────────────────────────────────────────────┘
```

Handel's *Messiah* performed at Salendine Nook Baptist Church, 11 December 1994.

Shiny pews and not a semblance of silly irreverent hand clapping and 'pop'. My mind returned to those *Messiah*s at Deighton Chapel, when mother and dad, smartly dressed for Sunday, sang in the choir. Shivers ran up my spine, not from cold – it was very warm – but the sheer majesty of the music. Brian Cooke was in the choir. His friend George played the organ.

The drugs Granville is having to take are giving him stomach pains – he couldn't stand up straight at times. Annie Whitwam 'phoned to enquire how he is. She has 'lost her faith' since her husband developed cancer. Though how she can blame God when Derek chose to smoke heavily all those years?

MONDAY 12 DECEMBER

9.50 p.m. Reading the paper when all the lights went out. Good job it was moonlight. Lit a candle then went to bed. Holding hands with Granville for a while, but he had violent indigestion so went into other bedroom. After an hour the lights returned, and Granville went downstairs to reset the outside security light.

Turn the switch off, count to six, then put it on again. Worried about contents of the fridge –and how would I know how to deal with such a dilemma if ever I was alone?

TUESDAY 13 DECEMBER

Very mild but dull. Put Christmas tree, borrowed from Edith, on table with all the extensions out. Decorated it while Granville went to the infirmary to see why these antibiotic tablets are making his stomach ache. Nurse told him they are awful for giving patients stomach ache, but do clear the infection. If he doesn't take the remaining pills it could flare up again.

Afternoon. Baked orange cake and a bran loaf. Then Granville made marmalade. All the windows steamed up. Had to open them. He has managed to fix first lot of coloured fairy lights and made them light. Feel quite amazed that he has done it without fusing the whole electricity.

WEDNESDAY 14 DECEMBER

First white frost. Washed tablecloth and hung it on icy clothes line. Granville to buy blu-tack to fix more Christmas lights up. Put royal icing on Christmas cakes. Granville ordered coal – £200 for a ton of coalite.

Afternoon. To Holmfirth in Beauty. Gave card to Bessie and Geoff Townend. Bessie had a cold so didn't stay. Granville bought two pairs of underpants in a factory shop, parsley in a greengrocer's shop.

THURSDAY 15 DECEMBER

Frosty. We were in middle of road after coming out of driveway and car refused to move. All the building site traffic lumbering past. Couldn't get through to AA on telephone. After half an hour or so Beauty decided to relent and take us to town. Crying when Granville said that a bus was flashing its lights at us – turned out it was doing it to another bus. In W H Smith's a lady asked if I would sign *Huddersfield in Old Photographs* to Mike, her brother. Home for lunch. Kept coat on so cold.

Afternoon. Typed letters to magazines then to Hampson's Garden Centre. Bought a long green trough for £4.10 to fill with green conifer boughs and red berries gathered on our Thurstonland walks. A thick green candle with snowman figure on cost 99p, a box of two decorated candles £1.25, four red candles 25p each and packet of flower seeds 89p. Probably to give as prizes on Christmas Eve.

There's a drought in Australia, yet there's been an abundance of rain here.

FRIDAY 16 DECEMBER

Made three jars of pineapple and apple chutney. Muriel Kelly rang. Would like a fridge in her cottage. Gas board told her walls are too thick to put wall heaters up. Good job they didn't say *she* was, I said, to make her laugh. Suggested she write a letter to *Choice* magazine about it. She may earn £15.

SUNDAY 18 DECEMBER

Early. lunch then to Upperthong to gather greenery and cones. Glorious fresh air and sunshine. Bulls in fields. One sheep looked to be lame. Spoke to them over a wall. Called to see Doris. The grey cat from next door inside with her, on the sunny windowsill. Someone has stolen Doris' holly.

Evening. Watched *Songs of Praise*, filmed in Huddersfield Town Hall with wintry outdoor scenes. Ada telephoned. Had to 'phone the emergency service. Couldn't lift Norman onto the stairlift to go upstairs. His legs 'had gone'. A coloured doctor came. Called Sareen. Ada kept calling him Doctor Sardine.

MONDAY 19 DECEMBER

Letter from Audrey. Hopes Granville better. Looking forward to reading my new book. She is having skin problems – could be caused by stress, her doctor said. Never been really fit since Philip died in 1978. And letter from Ian Emberson, the music librarian at Huddersfield. His novel-in-verse *Pirouette of Earth* to be published next summer. He misses Thurstonland now he has moved to Todmorden. 'Happy Christmas wishes from Ian, Catherine and Sooty.' Worst of Christmas is when no more post for days...

Big flakes of snow in the rain. Granville couldn't see to drive up Almondbury Bank – sun low in the sky after lunch. Usual walk. Days before Christmas often so much better than Christmas itself. Gathered holly and berries and arranged them in containers and in green wine bottles (empty) when no more vases. Upset to see photo of a horse carrying awfully huge weights of ammunition on either side of it, also on top of its back. Poor, poor thing. In Bosnia, taking it to the front line. They ought to shoot those who loaded the horse up like that. It had such a desperate look on its face. Even its head was dragged to one side with the enormous weight.

'Phoned Ada. Who always tries to console me by saying nothing lasts long – and the Lord is good. But while it does, it can be unimaginable agony. I know from that gall bladder operation!

TUESDAY 20 DECEMBER

Cold, fine and bright. Still sorting what gifts to give. Bought gloves for Caroline. Noticed when home 'specialist dry-clean only', so will have to take them back. (Always read the small print in future!) Saw a grubby, trembling-with-cold, little Jack Russell-type dog with a grubbier girl who was playing a carol on a tin whistle or flute. Quietly, in subdued manner. Awfully upsetting. Homeless, shivering, yet playing 'A Merry Christmas' to well-off passers by, when hers will probably be awful.

Oh, little dog and others like you, I pray to God that you will be looked after somehow, and that life will not be as bad and impossible as it appears to be.

Telephone rang. 'How did you get the picture of my husband on page —, because I'm his second wife and I didn't think it should be in, especially as it's his memorial this week – this is Mrs Hirst.'

What idiotic people I have to deal with! Told her Marjorie Stanley had lent it to me, and readers are pleased to see well-known local people in my books. Wished her a Happy Christmas and put the 'phone down.

WEDNESDAY 21 DECEMBER

Granville couldn't open car boot. It was frozen. Application of hot water and Beauty ready to go to Sainsbury's. Spent over £60 on groceries. Home for lunch. Lock had frozen again. We'd to put things on back seat. Wrapped more presents, washed rocking horse, vacced, Granville out delivering presents to Lesley and Donald Parkinson.

THURSDAY 22 DECEMBER

Perfect old-fashioned Christmassy weather. White, bright sunshine, freezing cold. Big lamp has conked out, so put it in back garden with a plastic container on top

Almondbury, Huddersfield. 'Better than watching television.'

as a container for bird food. Photographed it. Baked pastry cases for mince pies and vegetarian sausages. Washed Welsh dresser, polished it, put holly and plates back. Moved rocking chair in front room about a dozen different positions to see where it looked best. Granville cut geranium plants back and stored them in cellar.

Walk to Almondbury village. Gathered bits of wood, Granville complained I was 'mucking myself up'. At least I'm not buying a new dress from The Old Post Office – the name for the new fashion shop. Postman brought information about the Public Lending Rights for *Half a Pound of Tuppenny Rice*. 2p each time somebody borrows it from a library. It been borrowed so many times, £22.48 has been paid into Lloyds Bank.

'Phoned Audrey. Taking steroids has made her hair fall out. Has to wear a wig. Skin dry again all over her body. I've nearly finished knitting blue skirt. Caroline's friend Sheila thinks she is unsure about Richard.

CHRISTMAS EVE
White frost (what other colour?). Frantic last-minute preparations. Granville began washing kitchen floor wearing his best check jacket – ruining it – so I took over. He lit fires in both rooms.

Caroline, Richard and presents rolled in about 4.30 p.m. Granville went for Doris Lindley. I gave her a knitted red cap and matching gloves. Geoff and Bessie Townend arrived. Doris gave us two jars of homemade marmalade. Sherry first, getting to know one another – all blended superbly. Put nut roast, made this afternoon, in oven. Lentil and asparagus soup first. Candles on the table. Played games in cosy front room then to carol service at Almondbury Church.

CHRISTMAS DAY

Took breakfast to bed for Caroline and Richard. They then walked to Almondbury. Doris beckoned them into her bungalow, where they had sherry. Coffee here when they came back. To the Hilton Hotel, £45 each. Silly balloons kept snaking all over, rocket balloons or something. Afterwards Granville leapt out of car to get ticket for barrier and set off with driving seat door wide open. Called to see Ada and Norman. Gave them leftover mince pies and crackers to pull. Norman can hardly walk. He has a commode downstairs and was 'trying to make water', as he called it, when we went in. Gave Ada leftover turkey for the stray cat.

Richard wanted to watch *The Snowman* when we were back home. Because he used to every year with his daughters. He sat in the most comfortable armchair all the time, never once asking Granville if he'd like to change seats. Granville remained on the hard upright Windsor chair all the time. Pretending he was 'fine'. Preparing evening meal as we watched *Mr Bean* on TV. I could hear Richard's teeth clanking together.

BOXING DAY

Doesn't bear repeating.

TUESDAY 27 DECEMBER

Guests departed. House our own again. To Leeds. Parked Beauty outside Rackhams. Having an orange disability badge is a boon. Beauty can stay where others can't.

WEDNESDAY 28 DECEMBER

Wrote to Caroline at 5.30 a.m. Unable to sleep worrying about her.

Afternoon Feeling the need to talk. Granville and I to see Doris. She thinks Richard will go back to his family and daughters. 'Phoned Ada. It will cost over £300 a week if Norman goes into a Home. She also thinks Richard won't be loyal and 'looks foxy'. *Best of British* magazine has a review of my book *Pennine People*.

THURSDAY 29 DECEMBER

Typed letters. Looked at diary Caroline bought me. Saturdays and Sundays are on the same page, so will have to buy another. A lady telephoned to say my article about Sydney Pike is in the *Examiner*. Getting back to normality after Christmas, thank God.

FRIDAY 30 DECEMBER

Torrential rain. Mrs Shaw next door in a taxi to go to the doctor. Now widowed, can't drive, neither can I. Granville had offered to take her, but she said she doesn't want to be dependent. Took camera into Boots. Battery is finished, and can't get them like that now. To old camera shop on Queen Street. Bought another

Eighty-two-year-old widow Doris with Granville and Beth. 'Happiness is – the open air, a dog, a friend…' 30 September 1995.

camera for £275.99. Minolta, fully automatic. Tried putting a film in myself, but will never dare risk it. Granville does it – then I can't be blamed! Bought diary in W H Smith. It had a scratch on the front, so it was reduced to £7.99.

Caroline 'phoned at 5 p.m. Going to Special Constables. Didn't get my letter till this afternoon. Never mentioned contents. How much easier life is when people discuss matters. I'd go mad if I didn't. Yet Elizabeth and Caroline are like Granville, pretending problems will disappear if not mentioned. Just the opposite!

NEW YEAR'S EVE
Snowing intermittently. Doris said she'd walk here. Didn't want Granville getting stuck in car. When she arrived, a homemade Swiss roll was handed to me. It felt like a Second World War incendiary bomb, it was so heavy. Also a bright red silky scarf. That was alright. We all hope that by the end of 1995 both Elizabeth and Caroline will be in proper relationships, or at least not being mugs for married men.

Listened to music from Vienna when Granville returned from driving Doris and Marjorie home. New Year's Day began at 11 p.m. in Vienna.

'Phoned Marjorie to wish her a Happy New Year. Hate to think many are alone as Big Ben chimes in another year.

Ada's Christmas Eve

Jesus bids us shine,
With a pure, clear light,
Like a little candle,
Burning in the night
In this world of darkness,
So let us shine –
You in your small corner,
And I in mine.

Ada Truelove (as she was in 1926, aged nineteen), went carol singing with the Salvation Army in Bradley on Christmas Eve. She had a friend, Violet White, who was of outsize proportions. So much so that she had to wear men's boots when working in service at the rectory. Her clothes were protected with an ancient sacking apron tied around her ample form with black tapes. Ada thought her friend looked like the back end of a bus, but being a chapel-goer and brought up to be charitable, she put that thought aside and accepted an invitation to tea with Violet and her parents in a basement dwelling by the River Colne. Ada recounted the tale when Granville and I visited her and Norman with gifts of homemade mince pies and cake. We were never in the house more than two minutes before her stories of past years had us rolling with laughter.

Edith, Ada's sister, was also invited to the Whites'. As was Josiah Jackson, a local preacher. Mrs White had baked some date pasty. She put it outside by the drain to cool off. 'Nay, mother, you couldn't have put it in a more unhygienic place,' complained Violet.

Joyce Millos (née Lindley) and Ada Marston (née Truelove) in 1993.

'Right big was Mrs White,' recalled Ada. 'Twenty stones at least, with three big double chins.' Her husband, always known as 'Owd' White, was 'a bit lewd' and a ganger by trade, Ada confided.

Seated around the table, down that mucky sort of lane leading by the canal to some mills, Owd White grabbed hold of Edith's knee beneath the tablecloth. 'Well, you couldn't be in accordance with *that* sort of carry-on,' related Ada. So Edith made some excuse, probably a headache – and hurried off home. Mrs White hacked a piece of pasty for the parson (there were no niceties in that house) and Josiah Jackson began to choke, a date stone having lodged in his throat.

Ada, the only one with any presence of mind, thumped him on his back and when nothing happened tried to comfort the distraught man of God by assuring him that 'in the course of time and nature' he would part with it.

'Put your hand down your throat,' Ada suggested. But it was useless. He was unable to preach that evening. It was agreed that Ada, an occasional lay preacher, would give a little talk before the late-night carol singing.

The night was foggy, and all the gas lamps in houses had been extinguished in readiness for the Happy Morn. Owd White made a decision. 'Your father would be sickened if he thought you had to walk home in the dead of night,' he warned Ada as he adjusted the flickering gas bracket. 'You'd better off stay here with us. Violet sleeps on the horsehair sofa, so you can pig in with us.'

Although she had no means of sending a message home, Ada knew Herbert, her father, would understand that his daughter had been given sanctuary. 'But it was debatable which was the worst of two evils,' she said. 'Trying to make my way through a pea souper along the banks of the murky river, all alone, the Lord would not have wanted me to attempt,' she said, a Santa hat on her head. She had her usual little smile, which never turned into a frown, no matter what befell her. Besides, she was always mindful of never hurting the feelings of others. 'It would be like throwing kindness in their faces, so I took up Violet's offer of sharing a pull-from-the-wall mattress with her parents rather than the uncertainty of a foggy walk home that Christmas Eve.'

Ada had never pigged in with anyone before, let alone strangers, a married couple of gigantic proportions. But she dutifully went off into the night with the rest of the chapel carol singers, pausing every now and again for a glass of ginger wine and a slice of 'spice cake' at various hovels and cottages along the way. 'Many of the householders were blotto, it being Christmas Eve, and none of the singers were replicas of Caruso or Clara Butt,' recalled Ada. 'More like crackpots grovelling up and down. It was foreign to me, all that kind of carrying on.'

The Whites' was a one-basement room with a Yorkshire range, sink, sofa and a shut-away bed against the wall. With a glint in his eye, Owd White yanked it down. He didn't use a handkerchief very much and looked, according to Ada, 'sackless'. Both he and his wife had great big swollen legs, sweaty feet and creaky joints, and the bedclothes stank of wintergreen. It had saturated the blankets many moons ago. But they seemed happy as pigs in muck. She was handed a nightgown belonging to her hostess. So commodious that it wrapped around her slight form umpteen times.

Mrs White heaved herself onto the bed. 'You lie at the side of me, Ada' she said, indicating a few inches for the guest. Ada hesitated, but it was Hobson's choice. Pitch black outside, and once the gas was put out, the same inside.

Owd White told her there was a gazzunder under the bed in case anyone was taken short in the night, but Ada used the outside privvy before the Christmas Eve adventure commenced. 'Lying in between Owd White and his missus, I'd never have known whether to go right or left to find a gazzunder,' she continued while making us a cup of tea. Even at Christmas, alcohol was never given room in the household. But listening to Ada colourfully recalling every detail of that Christmas Eve in 1926 was intoxicating enough.

So Ada lay stiff, not daring to move, nay, not *able* to move between those figures snoring either side of her. The old overcoats chucked over the bed for added warmth meant Ada was as trapped as if in a jail.

'But everything passes,' she told herself as the hours moved slowly on to the Christmas morn. Members of the Salvation Army are taught to count their blessings. So Ada counted hers as she lay squashed between Owd White and his wife. She could walk, thank the Good Lord. That was *one* blessing.

When dawn came at long last her 'eyes felt like bullets for lack of sleep, and the frequent rattling in the chamber pot beneath the bed'.

'Did you have to go?' I asked Ada.

'Well, we know people *have* to go, given due respects, but I wouldn't have known which direction to take in that pitch blackness. Besides, thankfully, I was younger then, so the occasion didn't arise.'

She thanked her kind hosts for allowing her to spend the foggy night there instead of facing the dangers of the fog and canal. Then she made her getaway as fast as she could, walking home up to Father and Edith – to wish them a Happy, Godly Christmas. Mr Truelove pronounced the episode 'a bit of a dagger', in the parlance of the 1920s.

No modern stand-up comic with made-up lines could ever match the tales Ada Truelove told. Like her name, they were all true. She married Norman Marston when in her fifties, to do him a good turn. She would be his companion and housekeeper after his aunt died. Wife in name only. 'But we jog along alright don't we fairy?' she said to the morose, thin figure who sat opposite the jocular, ever-kind Ada.

They had to go into homes in the 1990s. Separate ones. 'We've looked at each other across these two armchairs for more than half a century,' explained Ada. 'Perhaps it's time we had a change.'

'But we'll be buried in't same plot of ground,' said Fairy, and they were.

Ada's sister, Edith, was born at the turn of the twentieth century. Herbert, her father, was widowed, eking out a living as a handyman on Yorkshire farms. And selling the occasional painting. Herbert, Ada and Edith lived at the old toll house on Bradley Road, near Huddersfield. A gentleman once offered him the opportunity to go to college in London, so impressed with Herbert's depiction of nature in his paintings.

He refused. Shallow city life was not for him. Neither was he interested in fame. He had a deep respect for 'the Word of God', and said that 'a person ceases to live in the true sense if he ceases to wonder and marvel at the handiwork of God'.

Four when she started school, Ada wore a garment cut down from a grown up's discarded coat. The teacher ordered, 'Take your coat off Ada.'

'I can't,' replied the awestruck child.

'Why?' demanded Miss Whoever-it-was.

'There's nothing underneath' explained Ada.

She and Edith never once thought of hanging a stocking up on Christmas Eve. But neither were they bitter about lack of presents. There were potatoes and turnips in the garden, and a huge holly tree up in the wood. They and their father could haul home branches laden down with deep crimson berries to adorn their cottage for Christmas. The children rejoiced with Herbert at the munificence of the woods. Especially when farmer Kershaw asked, 'Now Truelove, get me a couple of hares.'

After he had caught them, the farmer said, 'Merry Christmas lad – and take one home for yourself and little Ada and Edith.'

One winter, when winters *were* winters, a neighbouring farmhouse was snowbound for weeks. Mr Griffiths the coalman was unable to get through the drifts to deliver coal. Herbert was always ready to help anyone in trouble. There were small children in the farmhouse – they would be so cold!

'Leave the coal with me, I'll make sure it's delivered,' promised Herbert.

Ada and Edith watched in trepidation as the gaunt figure of their father – who suffered from epilepsy – set off bowed beneath a sackful of coal. They helped him over a wall, gasping in dismay as he sank from view beneath the snowdrifts. But up he came and ploughed a pathway through. The return journey with empty sacks was much easier. Often it's those with kindest hearts who seem to fare badly.

Another job was to wheel out an old lady in an old-fashioned bath chair. Ada christened it 'father's chariot.' The wheel at the front suddenly came into contact with a brick, and the old lady was catapulted into a bed of nettles.

Herbert was sacked, making the little family even worse off than before. But Herbert wanted to do the best he could for the little motherless daughters. Especially as it was Christmas. He wanted to give Ada and Edith a present each. Earlier, before the wheelchair catastrophe, the lady had given him a cast-off, ancient fur coat, bare in patches. 'He might be able to do something with it.' Herbert decided to make a Christmas teddy bear. He cut out the best bits, stuffed them with old rags, stitched it all together, and fixed a couple of boot buttons for the bear's eyes. That was for Ada. For Edith he had managed to get a little book, *Dollie Pie*.

The children slept beneath what had once been an Alhambra quilt, by then so patchy the original could scarcely be discerned. Firebricks were placed in the bed to warm it up a bit, and overcoats thrown over for extra warmth. When Ada and Edith were asleep, Herbert suspended the bear by a piece of cord from the bed rail. Later, when awakened by the sound of a brass band and carollers from the Salvation Army, Ada spied the 'monstrosity' hung over the bed.

'I couldn't have been more stunned if I had observed Sherpa Tenzing coming up the Himalayas,' she said to Granville and me one Saturday as she fondly recollected that childhood Christmas, causing us the biggest laugh of our own festivities many years later. But it was worth more to Ada than the most expensive toy a wealthier parent could give. She realised, child though she was, that it was meant to be a boy, and she was grateful to whoever had been so thoughtful.

'I carted my bear round with me for a long time.' It had, after all, been meant to please her. And the youngsters were grateful for whatever came their way.

Despite their poverty, they were happy and contented. Jesus the Saviour was born, and there were sticks in plenty to light the fire. Their father had even managed to buy some penny strips of green and pink crêpe paper from the top market in Huddersfield for his beloved little daughters to make into decorations.

Ada was never bitter about her childhood – the lack of material goods. It was overflowing in what really matters. Kind hearts, the beauty of the countryside in its different seasons. And perhaps best of all, a talented artist for a father, who could draw and paint pictures so true to life, she almost expected the birds and animals to move.

Christmas was where it should be – in the heart, not in the shops. And for me, those pre-Christmas days listening to an old lady describing, with humour, Christmases past, made Christmas all the more worthwhile. Indeed, throughout her life, Ada was a little candle, burning in the night. In a world of darkness, she in her small corner shone. And, like her Christmas bear made out of a mangy old fur coat, she will never be forgotten, because of the kindness and love bound up inside her.

A few years later, Edith married, and Violet White acquired a big fur – with a proper tail and head with glaring eyes – from a jumble sale.

'Is it a fox fur?' Ada asked with awe.

'Oh no, it's a goat skin with glass eyes put in to complete the picture,' said Violet proudly.

The clasp mustn't have been secure as it slid off when Violet heaved into the church and swept up the aisle. The person following, since his eyes were focused on the altar, ended up wiping his feet on it.

Violet had been entrusted with the task of making sandwiches for the wedding party beforehand. 'And more dropped on't floor than t'table,' moaned the bride's father. However, as always, the 'Good Book' was open on a small table nearby and all agreed 'it could have been worse'.

When eventually Owd White and his wife passed on to better things than shut-up beds and oil of wintergreen, Violet was free at last to become a wife. Her feet were still of outsize proportions, and no wedding shoes could be found anywhere, so there was nothing for it but to wear a pair of her late father's ancient white cricket boots beneath the white wedding gown. Nobody knew but Ada.

If Christmas is problematical, don't despair. Just remember 1926 in the West Riding of Yorkshire, and being in a shut-up bed with Owd White and his twenty-stone wife, and no heavenly scents of potpourri and pine cones, but an overpowering stench of stale wintergreen. Then you'll know for certain that Christmas could be worse. And if you have a storyteller among your guests, who can entertain with Christmas Crackers of the past, then you will have one of your best Yuletides ever. It isn't money that makes a memorable Christmas. Indeed, lack of it is often the key to sharing and knowing the true spirit of Christmas. Sharing – and caring. Happy Christmas!

Slaphappy

THURSDAY 21 DECEMBER

Frost-covered pavements and beginning to snow. In Beauty to take copy of *Huddersfield in Old Photographs* to Marjorie for Christmas present. I was given a white knitted toilet roll holder in the shape of a dog with its red felt tongue hanging out. From a church bazaar. How utterly stupid. After tea decided to walk to Morrisons supermarket at Waterloo. Then Granville couldn't find his Lloyds bank card. I started crying. Irresponsible twirp where money is concerned. What if all we've paid in has been taken by whoever has found it?

A youth and girl were jostling in an alley coming back. Granville shouted and was going to go up to them. He'd probably have been knifed. Home in disgruntled mood dragging trolley full of Advacaat, wines, and boxes of paints for Adele and Charlotte, £1.99 each. No use buying expensive ones until they are old as Abigail.

Caroline is giving me the *Writers' and Artists' Yearbook 1996*. I gave Mrs Shaw a copy of *Huddersfield at War*. Granville and I took it in turns to comb the pink rug, which has been washed and gone hard and matted. Slave labour.

CHRISTMAS EVE

Frosty, reddish, clear sky. Found four silver coins on floor by Granville's bed. Another year departing in the same slaphappy, irresponsible way. Usual stupid remark when reprimanded – 'I knew about them.' Why then doesn't he pick them up?

Making trifle and savoury scones, packing presents etc. Elizabeth, children and John arrived about 3 p.m. after leaving their luggage at the Hilton Hotel, Ainley Top. Vegetable stew. Abigail, Adele and Charlotte only wanted tomato soup. I'd made strawberry jellies as well as the trifle, leaving them without cream as they don't like it.

'It may not make my hair sprout – but
it could be a much-needed aphrodisiac.'
Granville's cucumber beauty treatment.

Evening. To Lepton children's carol service. Freezing when we came out. One
person's car door wouldn't open, so Granville sprayed de-icer on it. Abigail said I
looked like a Rastafarian in the green and red mohair beret.

Elizabeth tried some clothes on we'd bought for her. Black skirt a bit big, but a
friend can narrow it. She tried on the red velvet trousers. They fitted, but she didn't
like scarlet. Played scrabble. All compatible at long last. Wish we lived nearer
when so friendly.

Elizabeth uncertain about the way to Hilton Hotel. We are paying for all of
them. Easier than trying to make meals all eat! Granville went in our car with
her as far as Birkby Hall Road. I cleared crockery away, then we had late evening
service on television.

CHRISTMAS DAY

Bright, sunny, perfect weather for a Christmas morning, with snow on the
hills. Granville 'phoned the Hilton to suggest going for a walk. When he asked
if they'd had a good night, Elizabeth replied, 'I'll tell you later.' Jumped to the
conclusion something was wrong. I told him it would be that they were having
their breakfasts.

Took knitted caps for them to wear. Adele and Charlotte wanted the pom-pons
taking off or they would refuse to wear them. Talked to farmer feeding his horse,
Natasha. Graham Garside. His daughter bought *Pennine People* for his Christmas
present last year.

Charlotte and Adele, Christmas 1995.

Back to the Hilton about noon. Abigail put lipstick on the twins and has an eyelash curler! Kept warning them about wasting water as they kept it running when cleaning teeth. They wore longish black dresses and Abigail a pink shirt dress. Black velvet jacket used to be Caroline's, with black boots. Meal lasted from 1 till 3.30 p.m. The three of them came back sulking after there was no tinned tomato soup, although everything imaginable for 'starters'. Would have been cheaper to open tins of soup – and less annoying. Pauses in between courses. Natasha the horse was happier having her Christmas dinner out of a bucket outside. A conjurer dressed as Father Christmas kept coming to the table. The three of them were given selection boxes.

We came home first, to light fires in both rooms. The downstairs lights wouldn't come on. Granville went for Richard Armitage, but he couldn't come to see to them. He lent Granville a big torch as ours wouldn't light. After Granville had the whole drawer from the Welsh dresser out on the landing, looking for a fuse wire, the torch came on. Eventually, just before our guests returned, we saw the light again. By which time I'd lit candles – one fell over on the table in front room, so I had to put them in the fireplace for safety. Gave the rest of the presents, and Abigail drew a cartoon about Yorkshire water for competition.

Singing carols when Sheila telephoned. Upset because she'd been at her daughter's and an argument cropped up about which is the best wine. Gordon, the man she's been friendly with, turned awkward , and left after her daughter went to bed without even making a cup of tea. Sheila then at home apart from the cat. Quite a change for me to console somebody else after a family upheaval. John thinks our kitchen freezingly cold – which it is.

Abigail, Brian Duffy and Hazel at the Hilton Hotel, Huddersfield, 1995.

BOXING DAY

Perfect weather again. Picture book blue sky and sunshine, but piercingly cold. Caroline arrived at 10.45 a.m. just as we had retrieved a framed picture Granville had dropped down the back of a radiator. Narrow space to put my hand down while he was on hands and knees pushing it upwards. When it emerged and my hand was not stuck behind the radiator for the rest of the day, had a laugh. Caroline's childhood drawing, called 'The Hunt'.

Wore black velvet suit and green blouse. To the Hilton. John had been for a walk while Elizabeth stayed in the hotel watching Abigail, Adele and Charlotte in the swimming pool. Then Adele's trouser suit wouldn't keep up, usual carry-on in progress. We had to wait while those three applied make-up. Abigail accidentally jammed a mascara brush into Adele's eye. I said it was ridiculous wearing make-up at that age.

A jazz band was playing. Including Brian Duffy. Incredibly, he will be seventy next year. Elizabeth related about taking those three into Littlewood's once for tea. A row ensued – nothing new. Abigail stormed out, leaving her tea. I asked what happened next. Adele told me not to be nosey. Elizabeth didn't reprimand her, merely said, 'Let's change the subject.' Brian Duffy came across. Kissed me under the mistletoe. Then told me he'd just had flu.

1996

Helping at the Mission

MONDAY 23 DECEMBER

Frosty, cold, then rain. Baked sponge buns for trifle, also scones after being to Hampson's Garden Centre.

Bought two purple plants, £1.60 each, two red candles, 99p each, and small poinsettia plant, 75p.

Afternoon. Snow lining roads towards Thurstonland and on the distant hills. Took a purple plant and five packets of seeds for Joan and Harold. Alison, Gillian, Daniel and grandchildren there. Playing games, not watching television, thank goodness. We were given a bottle of whisky. Gathered holly on way back. Bit of sleet in the wind.

Evening. Knitting bed socks. Good programmes on TV for once. First World War and its aftermath, and a documentary about the magazine *Country Life*. Showed the editor and staff. Finally watched the somewhat maudlin *Love Story*.

Even so, before getting into bed, crying, and told Granville I don't want to leave him. Then remembered the £10 note I'd found on the bedroom floor – and told him he had never apologised about dropping that, and the other coins all over the place throughout the years.

One of the remarks in the film is 'Love is never having to say you are sorry' – which is quite wrong. Laughing, as usual, when we calmed down.

CHRISTMAS EVE

Up at 6.30 a.m. to avoid queues at Sainsbury's. Arrived before 7.30 a.m. Home before 8.30 a.m. Included in the shopping a net Christmas dog stocking for when Sooty is here on Saturday. Wrote to Rachel Henry. Elizabeth 'phoned. She and John have been to his mother's at Bexhill-on-Sea.

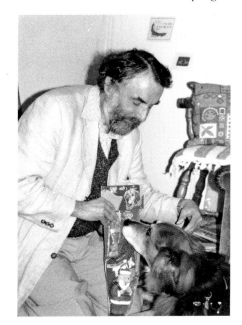 

Above left: Ian Emberson with Sooty's Christmas stocking.

Above right: 'Granville tries to get into the Christmas spirit by looping old necklaces over the banister – a distraction from problems of shutters that don't work and grandchildren who sulk.'

Cleaned all containers out for birds to water on garden path. Baked a chocolate Yule log after cleaning place mats and front room table. Non-stop. Sam, boy from next door, brought three wrapped bars of chocolate for Abigail, Adele, and Charlotte. After tea we watched King's College's 'Nine Lessons and Carols', and then I washed my hair. Too tired to trail out to a service, and too busy.

Richard Jennings has sent, by Interflora, a bouquet of red roses and white flowers for Caroline. On the card:

I hope Xmas was good. Egypt is a remarkable experience. Still have not been able to do joined-up writing nor find an Egyptian Princess. Hazel, you could write a book about Egypt and this 'Farouk'.

Happy Christmas, Princess, from Farouk.

Among the many Christmas cards, one which will be saved (in the diary):

With Best Wishes for Christmas and the New Year.

From Sutton Publishing Limited, Phoenix Mill, Thrupp, Stroud, Glos. GL5 2BU

Joyce, Peter, Liz, Lizzie, Rupert, Simon [and an unreadable signature].

CHRISTMAS DAY

Glorious weather. Granville flung dressing gown off in hurry to get in the bathroom, knocking jug of dried flowers all over landing carpet. At breakfast time before going to the Mission I said to Granville, 'How can Jesus be newly born every year for 2,000 years?'

Helping for first time at Huddersfield Mission to serve Christmas dinner to the lonely and homeless. We had tuna sandwiches and coffee in case we didn't fancy anything to eat.

One elderly lady wore a fur coat.

Talked with a vagrant who had a bag on the floor with all his belongings in it. He smelled, so kept my distance. He slept in an empty building last night. I asked what he'd do later. 'Walk about.' The unwashed stench was overpowering.

The chef, aged seventy-six, asked Granville to catch slices of turkey as he was cutting them up with an electric carving knife.

A big notice on a wall: 'It is illegal to carry a knife unless you can prove you need it.'

The minister said it was as well one person hadn't turned up 'as he had a low flash point'. The minister had intended saying Grace before the meal began, but some had already eaten the first course and were waiting for the main meal. One sent his plate back. 'Ah want one without Brussels sprouts.'

Christmas pudding was in long oblong foil wrapping, catering size. Cut into small oblongs. Cranberry sauce was left on most tables, so spooned back into the jars. One chap only wanted a bowl of custard, no pudding.

Going round tables with a plastic bag to collect leftover crackers, I asked a man from Primrose Hill, who had walked all the way there even though he'd had a stroke, if he wanted to put the fancy paper yellow cap on. 'I didn't know it was one,' he replied. So I put it on his head and asked if he felt warmer now. 'Yes, I do.'

A sign on a wall warned that no £20 or £50 notes could be accepted.

Then the man from Primrose Hill was in a panic. Didn't know where his house keys were, and couldn't remember if he'd locked the door.

A voice from the open serving hatch bawled out, 'Where are all the dessert spoons? I've already washed up a load – who's eaten the others?'

A lady wearing dark spectacles came to the kitchen and asked if I'd open a tin of prunes for her. She'd brought them as her body was allergic to wheat and Christmas pudding.

Many were smoking. They were fed up of waiting at 12.20 p.m. so had started long before Grace should have been said.

One dishevelled diner asked another in similar condition, 'Dusta want a drink o'watter lad?' He did. 'Good lad.'

Another asked, 'Are they pork sausages?' They didn't seem fully cooked – pale and insipid compared to the monster turkey. All went crackers for the gravy – huge jugs full of it.

The chef was William Grayson, 29 Ayton Road, Longwood. He'd peeled 16 lb of potatoes and had massive pans of vegetables, seemingly for giants, on the big oven. Told us when he was about ten, one Christmas Day, his mother said, 'Now *you'll* have to wash up.' And his wife was allergic to penicillin, so he learnt to cook. His mission in life apparently, was to be in the right place, Huddersfield Mission, that Christmas Day in 1996.

Talked to a sixty-five-year-old, fat, bearded, balding man. In a bright canary jumper. His best present ever a copy of the *Messiah* his mother gave him. And some Dinky cars.

An odd thirty-seven-year-old student (I'm nosey, always ask ages and all about people) announced he'd never had any presents. Wrote to the Queen twice, begging for money. Her Majesty wrote back, very sorry, suggesting he write to the Citizens Advice Bureau.

Another person asked for a cup of tea, a large one. But that wasn't served until later, when all went into another room to listen to the Queen's Christmas Message and 'finish off' with mince pies, coffee or tea.

The student told me he collects plastic white skeletons from out of the crackers – one of them must be his wife. Is studying microbiology, as well as being a cleaner.

Worst for the bright canary jumper wearer was the Christmas family party. He assumed the butcher had taken the giblets out of the goose. They were still there after it was cooked. So the cat had them. He is going to St Thomas' tomorrow for another free meal.

I asked the student what he was going to be. 'Qualified' the quick retort.

Canary Jumper said he didn't have white sugar. There wasn't any Demerara.

The garden of 58 Greenhead Lane, Dalton. 1996.

Daffodils in the snow, 14 April 1998.

When most had drifted away, a young couple came in and started to give a thinly clad four-week-old baby a feeding bottle of milk. They had a battered old pram, a thin sheet inside. Like the very essence of Christmas – only just 'room at the inn'.

What a start to life – a first Christmas among the poor, destitute, and often smelly vagrants. I copied the prices for normal days. Baked potato with grated cheese 95p, coleslaw 95p, baked beans 95p, cup of tea 21p, unbuttered scone 25p, buttered 30p, cup of Bovril 25p, beaker of Bovril 30p, glass of milk 19p, custard pie 25p.

'Helpers eat after the guests have finished,' we were told. Didn't fancy it, so came home to Greenhead Lane and gorgeous log fire.

Then *The Shepherds' Farewell* sounded on Classic FM. 'That's my funeral song, remember,' I remarked – and burst into tears. Worried if there was a burst pipe somewhere. A box of matches was soaked on the trolley outside the kitchen.

'If you go on like this they'll be sitting *you* down for dinner as well,' he replied.

Then washed the kitchen floor muttering, 'What a Christmas Day.'

BOXING DAY

Foggy, frosty. Elizabeth, Caroline and John arrived. Vegetable casserole in front room because sun gets in there. Herb bread warm from the oven. Had to open window, steamed up. Walk: Farnley Tyas, Almondbury, Sharp Lane. Talked to Wyn Turner's brother-in-law. His wife died not long ago. He looked a lonely, sad figure.

To see Dorothy at her daughter Sandra's. Her husband John there. Also Michael's father from Bridlington.

Home. Drink of tea and chocolate Yule log I finished icing this morning besides icing Christmas cakes. Presents. Gave John fur-lined slippers, gloves, socks and 'bath scrub' article. As he spends most of his life in the bath. Does at our house. Gave Elizabeth fur rug, bath towel, black velvet suit (only worn once, at Hilton last Christmas) and various other things. Green throwover for Caroline, vest, sheepskin gloves (gave Elizabeth a pair as well). The boots, she said, were too stiff, so will take them back.

All watched *One Foot in the Grave*. I slept on sofa bed in front room.